Faith, Healing, and Miracles

ALSO BY FREDERIC FLACH, M.D.

The Secret Strength of Depression

Resilience

A New Marriage, A New Life

Putting the Pieces Together Again

Rickie

The Secret Strength of Angels

Faith, Healing, and Miracles

FREDERIC FLACH, MD, KHS

HATHERLEIGH PRESS
New York

Hatherleigh Press
An Affiliate of W.W. Norton & Company, Inc.
5-22 46th Avenue, Suite 200
Long Island City, NY 11101
1-800-528-2550

Printed in Canada

This edition is printed on acid-free paper that meets the
American National Standards Institute z39-48 Standard.

Library of Congress Cataloging-in-Publication Data

Flach, Frederic F.
    Faith healing and miracles / Frederic Flach.
        p. cm.
    Includes bibliographical references and index.
    ISBN 1-57826-052-3 (alk. paper)
        1. Spiritual healing. 2. Miracles. I. Title.
    BT732.5 F537 2000
    231.7'3--dc21   00-027776

All Hatherleigh Press titles are available for bulk purchase,
special promotions, and premiums. For more information,
please contact the manager of our Special Sales Department
at 1-800-528-2550.

Designed by Dede Cummings Designs

10 9 8 7 6 5 4 3 2 1

Contents

PART IV
Healing and Prayer

PART V
Miracles of Discovery

PART VI
Faith and Resilience

Introduction

I BELIEVE IN ANGELS. I believe in miracles. And I believe that faith—by which I mean the extent to which people find their central motive in life in their relationship with God—profoundly affects our health and well-being. Not only does faith provide us with a world-view through which to understand and interpret all that we experience in life, but it also enables us to gain some sense of mastery in the face of circumstances that seem beyond our personal control. It gives us hope. It gives us the wonderful gift of prayer.

In this book, I have drawn upon these religious beliefs as well as my own expertise and experiences as a physician and psychiatrist to show how all of us may be able to develop and strengthen our intrinsic faith to serve us in our search for physical, mental, and spiritual healing.

After having written a book about angels with relative ease—with their help, I'm sure—I naively thought I could take on the task of writing one about faith, miracles, and healing in the same way. This did not prove to be the case at all. The amount of research required turned out to be enormous. To begin with, I found it necessary to extensively rethink much of what I thought I knew about miracles. Gradually, piece by piece, a new vision emerged. I realized that to talk about miracles I had to distinguish between those that were truly *extraordinary*, involving exceptions to the natural order of things—like those described in the Hebrew Scriptures, the New Testament, and, more recently, at Lourdes, France—and miracles that could best be categorized as *ordinary*. Ordinary, everyday miracles have nothing to do with the impossible. Rather, they achieve merely very improbable results. They involve the meaningful coincidences that can profoundly influence our lives and manifest the providential actions of God.

I can't say I've ever witnessed any extraordinary miracles. I really don't expect I shall. However, I believe I have come to understand their purpose more clearly, namely to amaze those who did witness them, thereby stimulating their faith in the power and goodness of God and, especially in the case of Jesus, demonstrate His great compassion for human beings. But I have seen any number of ordinary ones, in my own life, in the lives of both my friends and my patients, and I have read of many more in accounts of observers whom I respect and trust.

Being a physician, I've chosen to narrow my focus to miracles of healing, and to the role that faith and prayer seem to play in bringing these about. When I'd finished my research and completed my manuscript, I found myself far better informed on the subject than I had ever been. I also found myself greatly strengthened in my conviction that there is a personal God, that He loves us, and that He is always available to forgive, guide, protect, heal, offer us His friendship, and bless us in our challenging journey through life on earth toward eternal life with Him.

No authors can honestly say that they have approached their subject with complete impartiality. We necessarily bring to our subject matter points of view that reflect our deepest beliefs. But I believe that I could have written much of this book even if I were agnostic, for true agnostics are neither for nor against the existence of God and the human soul, but maintain open minds and hearts that stand prepared to entertain the possibility of meeting an angel or two and, in fact, God Himself.

But I am not agnostic. My personality and values have been strongly shaped by the Judaic-Christian tradition. I believe in God. I also believe that Jesus Christ is the divine Son of God. My faith in God is as strong as my faith in scientific fact.

As for prayer, the conversations we have with God, I can't imagine a rich life without them. This morning, at services, the Gospel reading was from Luke (11:5–10). It could not have been a more timely passage, reflecting my own thoughts and feelings as I sat down to write this introduction. Jesus relates the parable of a man who knocks at the door of a friend in the middle of the night to ask for food on behalf of another friend who has just arrived after a long journey. At first he is turned away. But when he persists in his efforts, his request is finally granted. Then, referring to the power and beneficence of God the Father, Jesus says:

So I say to you, Ask, and it will be given you; search, and you will find; knock, and the door will be opened for you. For everyone who asks receives; and everyone who searches finds; and for everyone who knocks, the door will be opened.

FREDERIC FLACH, MD, KHS

PART I

The Nature of Miracles

Mysticism keeps men sane. As long as you have mystery you have health; when you destroy mystery you create morbidity. The ordinary man has always been sane because the ordinary man has always been a mystic. He has always left himself free to doubt his gods; but (unlike the agnostic of to-day) free also to believe in them. He has always cared more for truth than consistency. If he saw two truths that seemed to contradict each other, he would take the two truths and the contradiction along with them. Thus he has always believed that there was such a thing as fate, but such a thing as free will also. It is exactly this balance of apparent contradictions that has been the whole buoyancy of the healthy man. The whole secret of mysticism is this: that man can understand everything by the help of what he does not understand.

Orthodoxy GILBERT K.CHESTERTON

1

The Mystery of Miracles

I AM EIGHTEEN YEARS OLD, lying in a Navy hospital bed, closer to death than I could ever realize, being only eighteen. Burning with fever. Trembling now and then with terrifying chills. Everything around me seemed as if in fog, clouded perceptions of human figures in white starched uniforms moving about. Coughing. Breathing hard. The feeling of firm but gentle hands up and down my back, cooling me, and the sweet aroma of rubbing alcohol winding up my nostrils. The sharp jab of a needle in my buttock. Welcome sleep.

I don't recall how many hours or days it took me to fully regain my senses. When I did, I saw, standing by my bed, the most beautiful woman I had ever seen. Her hair was light brown, her eyes a soft hazel, and she was smiling. I fell in love, instantaneously, being eighteen. Had I thought much about angels in those days, I might have mistaken her for an angel, but the thought never crossed my mind.

I looked at her more carefully, and discerned that she was, in fact, a nurse, a full lieutenant at that, and much older, at least twenty-three.

"You're going to be just fine," she said softly. "You've been getting a new drug, penicillin. A wonder drug. You've been very sick, with pneumonia. But you're going to be okay." She reached over and held my hand for a long moment. "It's a miracle, you know."

A miracle?

I've thought about this incident a number of times in the years that have passed since I was in boot camp at Sampson Naval Training Center, on Lake Geneva in upstate New York, in the bitter cold February of 1945, toward the end of the Second World War. I have always considered myself to have been the beneficiary of one of the amazing advances in medical science, which I learned about in medical school and have watched take place, first-hand, over many decades of medical practice.

Only now, as I've begun to consider miracles more seriously, can I see that what happened to me in that Navy hospital so many years ago could be considered a miracle, of sorts.

After all, what is a miracle? A wondrous event. We live in a world of wondrous events. I am writing this chapter on my word processor and when I have finished I will send it to my editor as an e-mail attachment, in an instant. Mobile phones, small discs that can hold movies made a generation ago for us to play on our television sets, and other wonders to which we've become very accustomed. Last spring, I flew from New York to Capetown, South Africa in a matter of hours. In today's newspaper, I read an account of one more miracle, Lance Armstrong's victory in the grueling bicycle race, the Tour de France. Armstrong is twenty-eight years old. Three years ago, he was diagnosed as suffering with a highly malignant and traditionally highly fatal form of testicular cancer. Inasmuch as the tumor had already spread to his lungs and brain, his chances of survival were practically nil. But he did survive, thanks to cisplatin, a new and potent drug, developed by Dr. Lawrence Einhorn at Indiana University. Armstrong's family believed it was an answer to their prayers. Armstrong himself called it a "miracle."

We doctors, of course, take a more skeptical point of view. We're trained to be that way. But before we draw any final conclusions, we ought to consider the nature of cisplatin and how it was discovered. Cisplatin was not found as a result of methodical scientific investigation. *It was found accidentally, the same way penicillin was discovered in 1929 by Sir Alexander Fleming.* Some thirty-five years ago biophysicists studying the effect of electric fields on bacteria observed that when a platinum electrode was used to produce the current, the microbes stopped reproducing altogether. "After much searching," said Dr. Jerome Groopman, a professor medicine at Harvard, as quoted in the *New York Times*, "it appeared that platinum had leached out of the electrode and poisoned the bacteria. The observation led to the study of drugs that contained platinum as potential inhibitors of rapid cell growth, the signature manifestation of cancer." Cisplatin contains platinum, and, in spite of having been tested against many types of cancer, it seems to work only against testicular cancer. "In less advanced cases than Lance Armstrong's," Dr. Groopman continued, "the cure rate is now about 95%." The only case of testicular cancer I saw was during the war, in a Navy fighter pilot who died within a short time after the diagnosis was made. "Armstrong's chances of survival, given his extensive bulky abdominal disease and the lesions in his brain, were estimated as not greater than 50-50."

Although Dr. Groopman speaks of numerous "medical miracles" occurring in the treatment of cancer over the past few decades—vincristine and prednisone largely curing childhood leukemia, nitrogen mustard and procarbazine for Hodgkin's disease, Adriamycin against certain kinds of lymphoma—I somehow doubt that he means any more by the word "miracle" than that a wondrous thing has taken place.

That's the way most of us use the word 'miracle.' A baby is born and we call that a miracle, especially if the mother has had a hard time getting pregnant or if the pregnancy itself was especially difficult. A highly intelligent, creative young man who barely passes his GRE examinations wins acceptance at a leading university to pursue his post-graduate studies in psychology, and he and his family refer to it as a miracle, an answer to prayer. A passionate gardener builds a special area for sick and ailing plants—she calls it a plant hospital—many of them seriously nibbled by rabbits and groundhogs, and when they bloom again, she refers to this as a miracle, a miracle of nature.

An old friend of mine gave me a slightly different slant on what he felt constituted a miracle. He had been a classmate of mine in medical school. He was a healthy skeptic, but someone who had always kept an open mind. Until his retirement, he showed excellent skill and remarkable care in looking after his patients. At first, he smiled at my mention of miracles. But as we went on, he suddenly recalled:

"Okinawa was two and a half months of hell. We lost 6,000 marines in that battle, dead, and thousands more wounded. Not to mention the army's losses and the sailors killed in the kamikaze attacks on the ships offshore. Just before our landing on the beachhead, I was sitting on the deck of the troop ship and thinking: 'If I get out of this alive, I'll become a doctor and spend my life helping others.'

"I was a sergeant. My men were killed all around me. I saw them carrying the bodies back on stretchers, dozens at a time. I knew my chances of surviving weren't good. No one's were. But I did make it through. And when I got back to the States and was discharged, I applied for med school and the rest is history. I've had a wonderful life. You could call that a miracle, I suppose."

Another friend of mine, Nancy, a woman in her early seventies, experienced her own sort of miracle. She had been diagnosed by doctors at Sloan-Kettering Memorial Hospital in New York as having cancer of her reproductive organs, with a life expectancy, even with treatment, of less that six months. She considered the gloomy outlook, and chose not go through the arduous therapy proposed. Instead, she called her stepson, a minister in a small town in Oregon, and asked him to pray for her. The minister, I was told, contacted all the other clergymen in the area and asked them to include my friend in their prayer services for healing, which they did. A few months later, when Nancy went for another medical examination, the doctors were astonished to find no evidence of her cancer.

A miraculous cure in answer to prayer?

The Latin derivation of the word 'miracle' is the noun *miraculum*, which means "a strange thing"; the verb, *mirari*, means "to wonder at"; the adjective mirus means "wonderful." The first definition of the word miracle in the dictionary is "an event or action that apparently contradicts known scientific laws and hence is thought to be due to supernatural causes, especially an act of God." I call these *extraordinary miracles*. I use the term *ordinary miracles* to describe happenings that are quite improbable, such as recovering from an illness when the doctors hold out very little hope for you, or completely unexpected coincidences that change the course of our lives for the better; coming upon insights into ourselves that lead us to become better people. In fact, the word 'miracle' is commonly used to describe the wonders of life, the birth of a child, the spring flowers blossoming, the hoot of the great owl perched high in a lofty locust tree, the earth itself and the stars above it. After all, these are truly marvelous things that would never have been possible but for the hand of God.

PART II

Extraordinary Miracles

What C.S. Lewis called the "snobbery of chronology" encourages us to presume that just because we happen to have lived after our ancestors and can read books which give us some account of what happened to them, we must also know better than them. We certainly have more facts at our disposal. We have more wealth, both personal and national, better technology, and infinitely more skillful ways of preserving and extending our lives. But whether we today display more wisdom or common humanity is an open question, and as we look back to discover how people coped with the daily difficulties of existence a thousand years ago, we might also consider whether, in all our sophistication, we could meet the challenges of their world with the same fortitude, good humour, and philosophy.

The Year 1000 ROBERT LACEY AND DANNY DANZIGER

2

Extraordinary Miracles in the Hebrew Scriptures

JOSEPH AND HIS BROTHERS

The Hebrew Scriptures, from the book of Genesis to the book of Malachi, are filled with prophecies and miraculous events. In Genesis, the story of Joseph tells how his brothers plotted to kill him. They were envious of the fact he was his father's favorite son. One brother, Reuben, suggested they throw him down a well rather than murder him. Another, Judah, on spying a caravan of Ishmaelites in the distance, suggested they sell him into slavery. And this they did, for twenty pieces of silver.

Many years later, his brothers had come to Egypt, first to buy grain, for there was a famine in their homeland, and a second time to reclaim a brother, Benjamin, whom Joseph had kept prisoner. By now he had become the governor of Egypt and chose to confront his brothers with his identity.

He said, "I am your brother, Joseph, whom you sold into Egypt. And now do not be distressed, or angry with yourselves, because you sold me here;

for God sent me before you to preserve life. For the famine has been in the land these two years, and there are five more years in which there will be neither plowing nor harvest. God sent me before you to preserve for you a remnant on earth, and to keep alive for you many survivors. So it was not you who sent me here, but God; he has made me a father to Pharaoh, and lord of all his house and ruler over all the land of Egypt." GENESIS 45: 4–8.

This is, perhaps, one of the earliest recorded examples of purposeful coincidence. Providence. God performing a miracle without violating the natural law. A series of circumstances, from the day Joseph was led off by the Ishmaelites to the day he welcomed his family to Egypt in their time of need.

MOSES

Just about everybody knows the miracles of Moses during the exodus of the Jews from Egypt. It is celebrated yearly in the Jewish feast of Passover. The rolling back of the Red Sea. The walking stick he used to tap the rock from which water then flowed. Manna in the desert. All signs of God's involvement, in spite of which even then the followers of Moses built idols to worship, stirring God's rage. It was not the first time God was described as being furious about human beings paying homage to false gods, and it would not be the last. In fact, throughout the Hebrew Scriptures, God's anger is repeatedly sparked by the failure to acknowledge his Oneness and to seek refuge and comfort in multiple deities: Molech, Baal-Peor, Astarte, Milcom, the gods from Syria and Sidon, Moab and Amnon and Philista.

God's communications with Moses are miraculous, as He reveals to mankind His guidelines for virtuous living.

The Lord spoke to Moses, saying:
Speak to all the congregations of the people of Israel and say to them: You shall be holy, for I the Lord your God am holy. You shall each revere your mother and father, and you shall keep my Sabbaths: I am the Lord your God. Do not turn to idols. . .

When you reap the harvest of your land, you shall not reap to the very edges of your field, or gather the gleanings of your harvest. You shall not strip your vineyard bare, or gather the fallen grapes of your vineyard; you shall leave them for the poor and the alien. . .

You shall not take vengeance or bear a grudge against any of your people, but you shall love your neighbor as yourself. . .

Do not turn to mediums or wizards; do not be defiled by them. . .

You shall rise before the aged and defer to the old. . . you shall love the alien as yourself, for you were aliens in the land of Egypt. . .

You shall keep all my statutes and all my ordinances, and observe them: I am the Lord. LEVITICUS 19: 1–37.

PROPHECIES

The dictionary defines the word prophet as meaning "a person who speaks for God, or by divine inspiration." And the Hebrew Scriptures are filled with prophets, predicting victories and defeats, reversal and good fortunes, of the Jewish people, dependent in large measure on how faithful they are to God.

NATHAN AND KING DAVID

The prophet Nathan, having communicated to David God's forgiveness of his crime of arranging for the death of Uriah the Hittite so that he could marry Uriah's widow, Bathsheba (David is forgiven because, in spite of his sinful ways, he has never abandoned his faith in and worship of God) predicts that, as a punishment, his son will die. And his son does die.

ELIJAH

Elijah, a prophet from Tishbe in Gilead, offers proof of the legitimacy of his prophecies by ordering the rain to stop in Israel, and warns King Ahab to mend his ways or be punished. Three years go by before it rains again. At God's request, Elijah goes to Zarephath to ask a widow there for some food. When she tells him she has none to spare, he performs another miracle.

For thus says the Lord the God of Israel: The jar of meal will not be emptied and the jug of oil will not fail until the day that the Lord sends rain on the earth. KINGS 17: 14–15.

Several days later the same woman's son dies. Elijah brings him back to life. The widow is astonished, saying:

"Now I know that you are a man of God, and that the word of the Lord in your mouth is truth." KINGS 17:24.

Elijah returns to Ahab, reprimanding him for worshipping Baal. He proposes a test. He and the prophets of Baal will compete to see who can make a fire appear under meat without actually lighting it. Baal's prophets fail miserably, and end up cutting themselves with swords and knives until they are bleeding, since this is part of their ritual. Elijah tells the people to pour water over the meat and wood, three times. He then prays to God, and the fire begins at once.

He offers Ahab a dire prophesy that is ultimately fulfilled.

"Thus says the Lord: Have you killed, and also taken possession?. . . In the place where dogs licked up the blood of Naboth, dogs will also lick up your blood. . . Because you have sold yourself to what is evil in the sight of the Lord, I will bring disaster on you. . ." KINGS 21: 17–23.

ELISHA

Elisha, another prophet, was with Elijah when a flaming chariot pulled by fiery horses appeared and took Elijah to heaven. Elisha also performed miracles in the name of the Lord, purifying water, providing jars of oil from a tiny bottle for a widow and her sons, predicting that a wealthy woman in Shunem would have a child, and later, when the boy died, bringing him back to life. The description of this event sounds a little like administering emergency cardiac pulmonary resuscitation, as Elisha stretched out over the dead body, with his mouth on the boy's mouth, his eyes on his eyes, and his hand on his hands, lying there until the boy's body became warm again. On another occasion, Elisha fed a multitude from some freshly cut grain and twenty loaves of bread, a miracle similar to that of Jesus as recounted in the New Testament.

Nathan was a commander in the Syrian army. He was afflicted with leprosy. He asked Elisha to cure him.

Elisha sent a messenger to him, saying, "Go, wash in the Jordan seven times, and your flesh shall be restored and you shall be clean. But Nathan became angry and went away, saying, "I thought that for me he would surely come out and stand and call on the name of the Lord his God, and would wave his hand over the spot, and cure the leprosy."

Nonetheless he went down and immersed himself seven times in the Jordan, according to the word of the man of God; his flesh was restored like the flesh of a young boy, and he was clean.

Then he returned to the man of God, he and all his company; he came and stood before him and said, "Now I know that there is no God in all the earth except in Israel..." 2 KINGS 5: 10-15.

ISIAH AND DANIEL

Isiah, another prophet, foresaw the captivity of the Jewish people in Babylon. Nebuchadnezzar, the king of Babylon, destroyed Jerusalem in 586 B.C. Daniel, also a prophet, was thrown into a den of lions for refusing to worship the king instead of his God, and was protected by an angel. Shadrach, Meshach, and Abednego also refused to deny their loyalty to God; they were thrown into a fiery furnace, from which they emerged unscathed. A fourth person was observed in the fire with them, most likely an angel.

Daniel also predicted the resurrection of the faithful at the end of time.

At that time Michael, the great prince, the protector of your people, shall arise. There shall be a time of anguish, such as has never occurred since nations first came into existence. But at that time your people shall be delivered, everyone who is found written in the book. Many of those who sleep in the dust of the earth shall awake, some to everlasting life, and some to shame and everlasting contempt. Those who are wise shall shine like the brightness of the sky, and those who lead many to righteousness, like the stars forever and ever. DANIEL 12: 1–3.

The prophets of the Hebrew Scriptures repeatedly urged human beings to walk in the way of God, and cautioned them of the terrible consequences they would incur were they to stray from that path. They warned repeatedly against listening to false prophets. In the words of Moses:

If prophets or those who divine by dreams appear among you and promise you omens or portents, and the omens or the portents declared by them take place, and they say, "Let us follow other gods, and let us serve them," you must not heed the words of those prophets or those who divine by dreams, for the Lord your God is testing you, to know whether you indeed love the Lord your God with all your heart and soul. DEUTERONOMY 13:1–3.

The prophets prayed devotedly to worship God and invoke His interventions. They used miracles to establish who and what they were. And while some of these miracles were pretty dramatic—such as hailstones falling on the Amorites, and the answer to Joshua's prayer that the sun might stop in the sky over Gideon and the moon stand still over Aijalon Valley until the Israelites defeated their enemies—many are simple, compassionate, and caring, providing food and water, healing the sick, giving hope to the least of persons.

While most of these miracles were extraordinary—manna in the desert, instantaneous healing of leprosy, bringing the dead back to life—others conformed to the laws of nature. No law of nature was violated in the events of Joseph's life. But the hand of God appears anyway, putting in motion a series of happenings that ultimately work to the good of Joseph and his family. We call this *providence*, a series of apparently coincidental events that lead to a conclusion that seems to have been intended all along for those who cooperate with God's will.

3

The Miracles of Jesus

THE LIFE OF JESUS was filled with miracles, everything from changing water into wine at the marriage at Cana to bringing Lazarus back to life. C. S. Lewis, writing about New Testament miracles, makes an interesting distinction between those of the 'Old Creation' and those of the 'New Creation.' The former involve sudden, local events that are not out of keeping with the nature of things as God originally created them. When Christ changed water into wine, for example, he is introducing a miraculous quality to an otherwise normal phenomenon. As the life source of the universe, God makes wine. "He does so by creating a vegetable organism that can turn water, soil, and sunlight into a juice which will, under proper conditions, become wine... Once, and in one year only, God, now incarnate, short circuits the process [and] makes wine in a moment."

The same may be said of ridding a man of leprosy or restoring his sight, in which a power to heal, already present within the individual's body, is miraculously activated. So too the calming of storms.

But not so for walking on water or bringing people back to life or His own resurrection from the dead. In these miracles of the New Creation, the very laws of nature are defied.

LAZARUS

Lazarus was the brother of two of Jesus' followers, Mary and Martha, who sent a message to Jesus, telling Him Lazarus was ill and asking for His help. When Jesus got to Bethany, where they lived, Lazarus had been in the tomb for four days.

"Lord," Martha said, "if you had been here, my brother would not have died. But even now I know that God will give you whatever you ask of him." Jesus said to her, "Your brother will rise again." Martha said to him, "Know that he will rise again in the resurrection on the last day." Jesus said to her, "I am the resurrection and the life, Those who believe in me, even though they die, will live, and everyone who lives and believes in me will never die. Do you believe this?" She said to him," Yes Lord, I believe that you are the Messiah, the Son of God, the one coming into the world." JOHN 11: 20–27.

Mary also came to Jesus and knelt at his feet.

When Jesus saw her weeping, and the Jews who came with her also weeping, he was greatly disturbed in spirit and deeply moved. He said, "Where have you laid him?" They said to him, "Lord, come and see." Jesus began to weep. So the Jews said, "See how he loved him!" But some of them said, "Could not he who opened the eyes of the blind man have kept this man from dying?"

Then Jesus, again greatly disturbed, came to the tomb. It was a cave, and a stone was lying against it. Jesus said, "Take away the stone." Martha, the sister of the dead man, said to him, "Lord, already there is a stench because he has been dead four days." Jesus said to her, "Did I not tell you that if you believed, you would see the glory of God?" So they took away the stone. And Jesus looked upward and said, "Father, I thank you for having heard me. I know that you always hear me, but I have said this for the sake of the crowd standing here, so that they may believe you sent me. When he had said this, he cried with a loud voice, "Lazarus, come out!" The dead man came out, his hands and feet bound with strips of cloth, and his face wrapped in a cloth. Jesus said to them, "Unbind him, and let him go."

Many of the Jews therefore, who had come with Mary and had seen what Jesus did, believed in him. JOHN 11: 33–44.

In restoring Lazarus to life, and later in His own resurrection, Jesus offered hope, and anticipation of another resurrection, our own, when the end times arrive.

MIRACULOUS HEALINGS

Most of Jesus' miracles described in the New Testament involve healing the sick in body and soul.

When they [Jesus and his disciples] had crossed over, they came to the land at Gennasaret. After the people of that place recognized him, they sent word throughout the region and brought all who were sick to him, and begged him that they might touch even the fringe of his cloak; and all who touched it were healed. MATTHEW 14: 34–36.

Again, at the Sea of Galilee:

After Jesus had left that place, he passed along the Sea of Galilee, and he went up the mountain where he sat down. Great crowds came to him, bringing with them the lame, the maimed, the blind, the mute, and many others. They put them at his feet, and he cured them, so that the crowd was amazed when they saw the mute speaking, the maimed whole, the lame walking, and the blind seeing. And they praised the God of Israel. MATTHEW 15: 29–31.

Christ seemed to make a point of confronting, irritating, and confusing the Pharisees by healing on the Sabbath by the pool at Bethsaida a man with a crippled hand, another who had been disabled for thirty-eight years, still another with swollen legs. Three of His specifically described healings restored movement and strength to crippled men; four involved restoration of sight to the blind, including one man who was blind from birth; two addressed leprosy, and in one of these healings, ten lepers were cured simultaneously; one restored hearing to a deaf man; and he healed Simon Peter's mother-in-law of a fever. A woman who had been bleeding for twelve years merely touched his clothes and was healed. We do not know what illness He miraculously cured in the servant of the official, but He did so at a distance, without ever being in contact with the man. At a distance, he also cured the son of a nobleman suffering with a fever. And he restored the ear of Malchus, which had been severed by one of Jesus' followers at the time of his arrest. There are also two more instances of bringing the dead back to life, Jairus' daughter and a widow's son.

His manner of healing took several forms. As a rule, He would simply say "you are healed" in so many words. But in healing the deaf mute, he stuck His fingers in the man's ears and put spittle on his tongue. For the blind man at Bethsaida, he placed spittle on his eyes and touched him twice. For another blind man, he used spit mixed with mud, and told him to wash it off in a pool of water.

FAITH AND HEALING

The issue of faith runs through all Christ's healings. He repeatedly points to faith as the context for miraculous cures.

One day, while he was teaching, Pharisees and teachers of the law were sitting near by (they had come from every village of Galilee and Judea and from Jerusalem); *and the power of the Lord was with him to heal. Just then some men came, carrying a paralyzed man on a bed. They were trying to bring him in and lay him before Jesus; but finding no way to bring him in because of the crowd, they went up on the roof and let him down with his bed through the tiles into the middle of the crowd. When he saw their faith, he said, "Friend, your sins are forgiven you." Then the scribes and the Pharisees began to question, "Who is this who is speaking blasphemies? Who can forgive sins but God alone?" When Jesus perceived their questionings, he answered them, "Why do you raise such questions in your heart? Which is easier, to say, 'Your sins are forgiven you,' or to say, 'Stand up and walk'? But so that you may know that the Son of Man has authority on earth to forgive sins," [addressing the paralyzed man, Jesus then said] "I say to you stand up and take your bed and go to your home. Immediately he stood up before them, took what he had been lying on, and went to his home, glorifying God. Amazement seized all of them, and they glorified God and were filled with awe, saying, "We have seen strange things today."* LUKE 5: 17–26.

Not only does this incident involve faith, it reveals the vital importance of forgiveness, so central to Christ's mission. Moreover, two of the purposes of miracles are demonstrated here: to incite the reaction of the crowds (their astonishment and acknowledgment of the power and goodness of God) and to show Jesus' great compassion for human beings.

When Jesus heals the two blind men who begged Him to have pity on them, He touches their eyes and says, "According to your faith, let it be done to you" And their eyes were opened. (MATTHEW 9:29) When he restores sight to Bartimaeus, son of Timaeus, He says: "Go; your faith has made you well." (MARK 10:52) When the woman who had been bleeding for a dozen years was cured after surreptitiously touching his clothes, he says, "Daughter, your faith has made you well; go in peace, and be healed of your disease.' (MARK 5:34) When, in Capernaum, he cures the army officer's servant he says: "I tell you, not even in Israel have I found such faith." (LUKE 7:9)

When Jesus healed the man born blind, his faith came to fruition after he had been cured. Here, Jesus also clarifies a very important issue when his disciples ask if the man's blindness had been the result of his or his parents sin.

"Neither this man nor his parents sinned; he was born blind so that God's works might be revealed in him. . . . As long as I am in the world, I am the light of the world." JOHN 9: 3–5.

A little later on, Jesus says to the doubting Pharisees:

"I came into this world for judgement so that those who do not see may see, and those who do see may become blind." JOHN 9:39.

The symbolic meaning of this miracle seems unmistakable, namely that one aspect of Christ's mission is to illuminate the hearts and minds of human beings, and that those who see and hear and still do not believe the will of God, do so at their own peril.

THE PURPOSE OF MIRACLES

Some Christians believe that miracles in general, and those of Jesus in particular, were meant only to call attention to and confirm the validity of God's revelations. But others, myself included, feel that they were meant to demonstrate Jesus' compassion for the vulnerabilities of human kind, our susceptibility to disease, the inevitability of death—and so stir our own compassion and abilities to heal another.

The value of miracles is not limited to their role in confirming religious truths," wrote philosophers and theologians R. Douglas Geivett and Gary R. Habermas in *In Defense of Miracles.* "If we seriously allow that God is a personal agent who acts in human history, we must allow that God may have other purposes for producing miracles. It may even be that the evidential value of miracles is secondary to the value they have in addressing the needs of human beings . . . a testimony to the compassion of God for human beings benighted by sin and circumstance."

THE ACTS OF THE APOSTLES

After the four gospels of Matthew, Mark, Luke, and John, the Acts of the Apostles, written by Luke, tells the story of the efforts of Christ's followers to spread His message to Jews and Gentiles alike, from Christ's ascension into heaven and the coming of the Holy Spirit on Pentecost to Paul's arrival in Rome. The Acts are filled with miracles. *'Awe came upon everyone, because many wonders and signs were being done by the apostles.'* (ACTS 2:43) Peter and John are described healing a lame man (ACTS 3:1-10). Philip went to Samaria and told the people about Christ. *"The crowds with one accord listened eagerly to what was said by Philip, hearing and seeing the signs that he did, for unclean spirits, crying with loud shrieks, came out of many who were possessed; and many others who were paralyzed or lame were cured."* (ACTS: 8: 6-7)

Peter healed Aeneas, who had been ill and confined to bed for eight years, and many people who saw the recovered Aeneas became followers of the Lord. In Joppa, a Christian named Tabitha, who had always been generous to the poor, had died. Peter was sent for. He came and knelt by her body and prayed, and when he told her to rise, she did. Once again, as this became known throughout Joppa, *many believed in the Lord.* ACTS 9:36-42 An angel rescued Peter from prison. (ACTS 12:6-12) Barnabas and Saul struck blind a man called Bar-Jesus who practiced witchcraft and was a false prophet in the city of Paphos.(ACTS 13: 4-12)

In Lystra a man who had been born with crippled feet and had never been able to walk was listening to Paul speak. When Paul saw that he had faith in Jesus and could be healed, he told the man to stand up and walk, which he promptly did. (ACTS 14: .8-10) In Troas, Paul revived a young man named Eutychus who had been killed in a fall. (ACTS 20: 7-12) On the island of Malta, the father of Publius, sick with fever and stomach problems was healed when Paul placed his hands on him and prayed. (ACTS 28: 7-8)

MIRACLES SINCE THE TIME OF THE APOSTLES

Some Christians believe the age of miracles ended with the death of the last apostle. But others believe that they have been occurring all through the centuries, in association with the lives of men and women who appear to have been especially devout in the service of God, whom some call saints. Substantial evidence of miracles hav-

ing occurred in connection with a prospective saint is one requirement of the Catholic Church for the canonization of such figures as
St. Francis of Assisi, St. John of the Cross, St. Teresa of Avila, St.
Bernadette of Lourdes, and St. Peregrine, the patron saint of spontaneous cancer regression. A fourteenth century priest, Peregrine
was awaiting the next day's amputation of his foot because of a cancerous growth. He prayed. In his sleep, he dreamed he was cured.
And when he awoke, indeed he was cured, and he lived to be eighty
years old.

It might be easier for us to acknowledge the reality of miracles if
we were to see the kind of spectacular happenings recounted in the
pages of the Hebrew Scriptures and the New Testament, if we could
witness Lazarus coming out of the tomb or the instantaneous healing
of the ten lepers. Of course, not everyone who witnessed these events
believed in them. But perhaps our acceptance of them would no
longer have to be a matter of faith. We would know that they exist.
But that's not likely to be the case for most of us. I have certainly
never seen a miracle that clearly defies the natural order of things. No
one I know has either. And considering what C. S. Lewis observed
about such extraordinary miracles, perhaps that's just as well:

*"You are probably quite right in thinking that you will never see a mir-
acle done* [in the extraordinary sense, involving a breech in the laws of
nature]; *you are probably equally right in thinking that there was a natural explanation of anything in your past life which seemed, at the first
glance, to be "rum" or "odd." God does not shake miracles into Nature at random as if from a pepper-caster. They come on great occasions; they are found
at the great ganglions of history—not of political or social history, but of
that spiritual history which cannot be fully known by men. If your own life
does not happen to be near one of those great ganglions, how should you expect to see one? If we were heroic missionaries, apostles, or martyrs, it would
be a different matter. But why you or I? Miracles and martyrdoms tend to
bunch about the same areas of history—areas we have naturally no wish to
frequent."*

But is it possible that we are now living in such a "ganglion of spiritual history"? Have events of the past two centuries moved toward a climactic struggle between good and evil, forces of light and darkness? Has an age of miracles returned to earth, to amaze us, frighten us, arrest our attention, bring us to our knees, asking us to reconsider what we value, where we have come from and where we are headed in the millennium before us?

4

Marian Apparitions

MARY, THE MOTHER OF JESUS, has been a central figure in many Christian religions, though not all. Moslems have a special reverence for her as well. Although they do not believe in Christ's divinity and deny his resurrection, nonetheless they remain convinced that Jesus was conceived to a virgin and view this as a miraculous event.

Many of the reported appearances of Mary over the centuries deserve to be regarded with healthy skepticism at best. However, several of these appear to be more verifiable. While many Christians, especially Catholics, do look upon them as real, they are by no means required to do so as part of their religious faith. Nonetheless, they deserve our attention for two reasons, first because unusual healings have been associated with them, and second, because Mary's consistent plea is for all human beings to strengthen their faith in God through prayer.

On April 2, 1968, a mysterious and beautiful woman clothed in garments that "shone like the noonday sun" appeared atop Saint Mary's Coptic Orthodox Church in Zeitoun, Egypt, a suburb of

Cairo, to the astonishment of a group of transport workers passing by. One of them, Farouk Mohammed Atwa, who had a gangrenous finger that was to be amputated the following day, was healed as he stood there gazing at the apparition. A week later, the same vision was sighted and it is estimated that about 250,000 people, Muslims and Christians alike, saw it return again and again over the next three years. The Patriarch of the Coptic Church, Kyrillos VI, publicly stated that he had no doubt whatsoever that the woman was Mary, the Mother of God, and a spokesman for the local Protestant denominations agreed. Although Mary never spoke, it was generally assumed that her appearance to people of so many different faiths was a clear sign that all prayer is precious to God, since he is Father to all, and heartfelt prayer is the universal language of love.

MEXICO CITY, MEXICO, 1531

In 1531, Mary is believed to have appeared to a fifty-seven year old Aztec Indian, a convert to Christianity, Juan Diego, on Tepayac Hill, then a barren desert, but at one time the site of a temple to the mother-goddess of the Aztecs. Speaking to him in his native language, surrounded by brilliant rays of light, she identified herself as the "Mother of the true God who gives life and maintains it in existence. He created all things. He is in all places." She instructed Juan Diego to tell the local bishop that she wished a church built at this place. He did as he was told, but the bishop was not entirely impressed.

When he saw her again, she asked him to gather a huge array of Castillian roses, which were quite unlikely to be found there, wrap it in his mantle, and take it to the bishop. When Juan Diego opened his cloak in front of the bishop and his staff, they were astonished by the roses, but even more so by the full-length image of Mary mysteriously imprinted on the fabric. The mantle still hangs on display in the basilica on Tepayac Hill in Mexico City. Millions of pilgrims have visited this shrine in search of hope, and sometime miracles.

LA SALETTE, FRANCE, 1846

True prophecies are considered to be a form of miraculous communication. In 1846, Mary is believed to have appeared to two children, Melanie Mathieu age fourteen and Maximin Giraud, age eleven, in La Salette, France, high in the French Alps. She warned of a serious famine to come, and appealed for them to make known God's wish that people would once again place their faith in Him. A spring of water was discovered in the place where this occurred, and miracles of physical healing began to be associated with the water; several blind people reportedly regained their sight when they bathed their eyes in it, and a number of disabled people were able to walk again.

Famine was not the only prophesy that came to pass. When the Pope learned the secret confided to Maximin, he commented: "There are scourges that menace France. Germany, Italy, all Europe is culpable and merits chastisements." The Franco-Prussian War was only twenty-four years away, World War I sixty-eight years, and World War II ninety-three. In fairness, the historical proclivity of human beings for internationally sanctioned slaughter, would make such a prediction very likely to be fulfilled

There was another, even more chilling prophesy reportedly conveyed at La Salette.

"In the year 1864, Lucifer together with a large number of demons will be unloosed from hell: they will put an end to faith little by little . . . Evil books will be abundant on earth and the spirits of darkness will spread everywhere, a universal slackening in all that concerns the service of God . . . only homicides, hate, jealousy, lies and dissension will be seen without love for country or family . . . The righteous will suffer greatly. Their prayers, their penances and their tears will rise up to Heaven . . . then Jesus Christ, in an act of His justice and His great mercy, will command His angels to have all His enemies put to death . . . all those given over to sin will perish and the earth will become desert-like. And then peace will be made, and man will be reconciled with God . . . "

FATIMA, PORTUGAL, 1917

Another appearance occurred in Fatima, Portugal in 1917. Here Mary is said to have appeared to three children, Lucia, eight, Francisco, seven, and Jacinta, five, urging prayer by means of the rosary.

The first appearance took place on May 13, and recurred for six months on the thirteenth of each month. On July 13, Mary promised a cosmic miracle to convince people of the reality of her presence and the urgency of her messages. She also predicted the end of World War I, but warned that another war would follow. Furthermore, if concerted efforts at prayer were made, Russia, then in the agony and violence of the Bolshevik revolution, would return to God.

The promised miracle occurred on October 13. Before thousands of pilgrims the sun shook and spun so fiercely it seemed to explode and come down toward the frightened onlookers. Suddenly it stopped and returned to its normal place in the sky.

On October 13, 1973, in Akita, Japan, fifty-six years after Fatima and twenty-eight years following the atomic bombing of Hiroshima and Nagasaki, Mary is said to have appeared to a Catholic nun, Sister Agnes Katsuko Sasagawa, echoing the predictions made at Fatima:

"If people do not repent and better themselves, God the Father will allow a terrible punishment of their own making to fall upon them. All humanity will be involved. It will be a punishment greater than the deluge . . . Fire will fall from the sky and will wipe out a great part of humanity."

How much faith should we have in such reports of Marian apparitions? Should any of us believe in these appearances of Mary and the prophecies associated with them? Even the Catholic Church, which is most closely associated with these events, makes quite clear that they do not deserve the same level of theological faith that is due the revelations made known through the Bible. Pope Benedict XIV, writing about the partially approved revelations of Saint Hildegarrde, Saint Bridget, and Saint Catherine of Sienna, stated authoritatively that " . . . those revelations, although approved of, ought not to, and cannot, receive from us any assent of Catholic [faith], but only of human faith, according to the rules of prudence, according to which the aforesaid revelations are probable, and piously to be believed in." Does that mean there can be room for error in these many revelations? Does it mean that even a devout Christian does not have to believe in any or all of Mary's supposed appearances, even those said to have taken place at Lourdes?

Fr. Benedict J. Groeschel, in *A Still Small Voice*, offers this answer: "I *think* that Lourdes is a special gift of God to us all." As someone deeply devoted to this shrine and to Saint Bernadette and as one who has a very strong opinion that it all happened as the little peasant saint said, it pains me to admit that you do not have to accept the apparition at Lourdes if, after studying the fact, you decided not to. (I reserve the right to think you are foolish if you don't.) The recipient of the vision can make mistakes. Saint Catherine Laboure actually predicted the bloody disturbances of the French Commune forty years before they occurred and with the precise date. She made a number of other predictions that were wrong. When confronted with these errors, she simply apologized for getting the facts of the revelation wrong.

5

Lourdes, France, 1858

THE REPORTED APPEARANCE of Mary to Bernadette Soubirous at Lourdes, France, demands our special attention, since here, as nowhere else, hundreds, perhaps thousands of miraculous healings are said to have taken place.

In 1858, a sickly young girl of eleven, Bernadette Soubirous, experienced eighteen appearances of Mary. She was given three secrets, which she never revealed.

"Suddenly I heard a great noise," Bernadette later wrote, "like the sound of a storm. I looked to the right, to the left, under the trees of the river, but nothing moved. I thought I was mistaken . . . Then I heard a fresh noise like the first. I was frightened and stood straight up. I lost all power of speech and thought when, turning my head toward the grotto, I saw at one of the openings of the rocks a rosebush, one only, moving as if it were very windy. Almost at the same time there came out of the interior of the grotto a golden colored cloud, and soon after a Lady, young and beautiful, exceedingly beautiful, the like of whom I had never seen, came and placed herself at the entrance of the opening above the rosebush. She looked at me immediately, smiled at me and signed to me to advance, as if she had been my Mother. All fear had left me but I seemed to know no longer where I was. I rubbed my eyes, I shut them, I opened them; but the Lady was still there continuing to smile at me and making me understand that I was not mistaken. Without thinking of what I was doing, I took my Rosary in my hands and went on my knees."

Bernadette was asked to pray for sinners. During one of her apparitions, presumably following instructions, the young girl dug in the mud until, first a trickle, then a gush of water flowed from the site. She was asked by Mary to communicate a request to have a chapel built there, where the sick could come as a sign of their faith and hope in God's love and mercy. After these experiences, Bernadette retired to a convent in Nevers, where she died of tuberculosis at the age of thirty-five, a very young age for these days, but not too far away from the average life expectancy for the middle of the nineteenth century.

In the nearly 150 years since then, millions of pilgrims have visited the shrine, and thousands are said to have been miraculously healed of their illnesses. What makes Lourdes especially relevant to any discussion of miracles is that many of these cures have been carefully studied. At least 2,000 of them have been classified as extraordinary, inexplicable by physicians. Between the first cure, that of Catherine Latapie in March of 1858 to the most recent, that of Msgr. Jean Orchampt in June, 1978, more than sixty have been approved by the Catholic church as "truly miraculous."

There is a strict protocol for declaring a cure at Lourdes a miracle.

- First, it must be proved that an illness existed and a medical diagnosis must be established. Furthermore, it must be clear that the patient's prognosis, with or without treatment is poor; the illness must be serious and incurable by known methods.
- The cure must be instantaneous; it must take place within a matter of hours or, at most, a few days.
- And it must be permanent, to distinguish it from a temporary remission of the condition.

• Finally, it must be approved by the Medical Bureau of Lourdes, the diocese where the cured person resides, and the Church in Rome.

It is interesting to review the kinds of approved miraculous cures that have occurred at Lourdes, and the people who were the beneficiaries of these healings. Of sixty-four cases, fifty-three (86%) were French, the remaining eleven (14%) came from several other European countries. Fifty-three (83%) were women; eleven (17%) were men. Only ten (17%) were members of religious orders. The majority of conditions cured—twenty-nine (45%) involved advanced forms of tuberculosis, affecting not only the lungs, but the nervous system and bone as well. Seven cases were afflicted with abscesses or infections other than tuberculosis, five with diseases of the central nervous system, four with serious injuries resulting from accidents, four with gastrointestinal ailments, three with cancer, and one each with liver disease, renal disease, ulcers, Addison's Disease, or spinal arthritis, and one with a rare case of Bud-Chiari disease affecting the portal veins of the liver. In the setting of these other diseases, two had become blind, and a third was blind from birth.

THE JOURNEY OF ALEXIS CARREL

Alexis Carrel, a world famous medical researcher, wrote a remarkable report on his visits to Lourdes, entitled *The Voyage to Lourdes*, published posthumously in 1950 four years after his death. Carrel was born in France in 1873. He received his medical degree from the University of Lyons. Although raised Catholic, as a student and later as a physician, he become a confirmed agnostic, committed only to the validity of scientifically established facts.

Carrel was the first to develop the art of reconnecting ruptured blood vessels (1902). He even kept alive a small tissue taken from the heart of an embryo chick, which actually outlived Carrel himself, after he himself died in 1944. Much of his research was carried out at the Rockefeller Institute in New York. During the 1920s, he collaborated with Charles Lindbergh to develop a heart-pump, which would prove vital for future cardiac surgery and organ transplants. In 1912 he was awarded the Nobel Prize in medicine.

In 1903, as a favor for a colleague, Carrel volunteered to accompany a group of seriously ill people traveling to Lourdes. While there, he witnessed the cure of a twenty-three year old woman, Marie-Louise Bailly, who was on the point of dying of tubercular peritonitis. While still in the sanitarium, prior to her pilgrimage to Lourdes, she believed that she would be cured; she said that Mary herself had inspired her to have such faith: "The more often the doctors declared that I would soon die, the greater faith I had that I would be cured. The Holy Virgin obtained that grace for me because she knew that my cure would effect the conversion of a person whose unbelief made me suffer more than all my ills."

En route to Lourdes, Marie Bailly and Dr. Carrel shared the same train, affording him the opportunity to see just how gravely ill she was. When they arrived in Lourdes on May 27, 1903, she was practically unconscious. The next day, she was carried to the baths. "I asked the nurse to apply the water again," she later recalled. "She agreed. It was then that I felt that a miracle was taking place in me. As much as the first application of water gave a painfully burning sensation, the second felt like sweetness itself. My chest, which until then rose only with difficulty, began to emit long sighs. Dr. Carrel, who stood by, watched with astonishment the flight of the sickness while he was jotting notes on his cuffs." By May 30, Marie was incredibly stronger and able to return home.

Carrel prepared a deposition of what he had seen for the Medical Bureau of Lourdes. However, he remained far from certain as to how to interpret the events he had witnessed. He continued to be interested in the reported miracles at Lourdes from a scientific perspective. He wrote: "For a long time physicians have refused to study seriously the cases of miraculous cures. They have disregarded the fact that it is a huge scientific error to deny facts before examining them."

Carrel returned to Lourdes four times between 1908 and 1912. During his 1912 visit he observed another miraculous cure, the sudden restoration of vision in an eighteen-month-old child who had been born blind.

He remained unconvinced. In 1935 in *Man the Unknown*, he asserted that the practice of Christian virtues seemed to him essential for man's survival, but he avoided assigning these a supernatural origin. He still considered the sudden and inexplicable cures occuring at Lourdes as having a natural explanation, although not one that could, as yet, be discerned by contemporary medical science.

Describing healing miracles Carrel wrote: "The process of healing changes little from one individual to another. Often an acute pain. Then a sudden sensation of being cured. In a few seconds, a few minutes, at the most a few hours, wounds are cicatrized, pathological symptoms disappear, appetite returns. Sometimes functional disorders vanish before the anatomical lesions are repaired. The skeletal deformation of Pott's disease, the cancerous glands, may still persist two or three days after the healing of the main lesions. The miracle is chiefly characterized by an *extreme acceleration of the processes of organic repair*' [ital. add.].

Based on his inquiries and observations, he concluded: *"There is no need for the patient himself to pray, or even to have any religious faith. It is sufficient that someone around him be in a state of prayer.* Such facts are of profound significance. They show the reality of certain relations, of a still unknown nature, between psychological and organic processes. They prove the objective importance of the spiritual activities, which hygienists, physicians, educators, and sociologists have almost always neglected to study. They open man to a new world."

Carrel remained agnostic much of his life. But in 1942, two years before his death, he wrote in his diary: "I believe in the existence of God, in the immortality of the soul . . . " A few days before his death he said: "When one approaches one's own death, one grasps the nothingness of all things. I have gained fame. The world speaks of me and of my works, yet I am a mere child before God, and a poor child at that."

As Marie-Louise Bailly said, "'. . . *my cure would effect the conversion of a person whose unbelief made me suffer more than all my ills.*" Perhaps the cures Carrel witnessed effected the rebirth of his own faith.

Casablanca, starring Humphrey Bogart and Ingrid Bergman, won the Academy Award as the best film of 1943. But another movie was nominated for twelve Academy Awards. Jennifer Jones won the Oscar for leading actress, Arthur Miller for cinematography, James Bosevi, William S. Daly, and Thomas Little for art direction/black and white, and Alfred Newman for musical scoring of a dramatic presentation. *The Song of Bernadette*, based on the best-selling novel of the same name by Franz Werfel, was a marvelous tribute to the astonishing events that had taken place at Lourdes nearly a hundred years earlier. There's a familiar line in the screenplay, spoken by Charles Bickford, who plays the village priest. In the background, throngs of people are milling through the village on their way to Bernadette's shrine. Vincent Price, playing the part of a former town official and a recalcitrant skeptic, makes a derogatory remark about them. Bickford chides him, replying: "For those who believe, no explanation is necessary. For those who do not, none will suffice."

'For those who believe . . . ' Once again, faith is the issue, and a perplexing one at that. True, methodical investigations have been carried out to verify the reality of the miracles at Lourdes. Like Alexis Carrel, many people, have witnessed them for themselves. But still, a leap of faith seems to be necessary to accept these events. Haunting questions remain. Why, if there is a personal God, does He so gradually reveal Himself to human beings? Why in such a mysterious way? Why does He demand that we place our trust in Him, with apparently so little tangible evidence for His presence in our lives?

Perhaps miracles are tests of our faith. Belief in miracles, like belief in God, involves a leap of faith. Let's not forget that thousands of people saw the manna from heaven in Moses' time, Elijah setting afire the water-soaked wood and pointing up the impotence of the prophets of Baal, Shadrach, Meshach, and Abednego and emerging from the fiery furnace unscathed. Thousands more saw Jesus heal the sick and drive out demons. And again, thousands have known first-hand of the healings at Lourdes. Yet many of these witnesses re-mained unconvinced, or if impressed, too threatened by the implications of what they had witnessed to accept the reality and meaning of it.

PART III

Miracles
in
Everyday Life

Annie has pulled Helen downstairs again by one hand, the pitcher in her other hand, down the porch steps, and across the yard to the pump handle, grimly.

Annie: All right. Pump. (Helen touches her cheek, waits uncertainly.) No, she's not here. Pump! (She forces Helen's hand to work the handle, then lets go. And Helen obeys. She pumps till the water comes, then Annie puts the pitcher in her other hand and guides it under the spout, and the water tumbling half into and half around the pitcher douses Helen's hand. Annie takes over the handle to keep water coming, and does automatically what she has done so many times before, spells into Helen's palm:) Water. W, a, t, e, r. Water. It has a name (And now the miracle happens. Helen drops the pitcher on the slab under the spout, it shatters. She stands transfixed. Annie freezes on the pump handle; there is a change in the sundown light, and with ita change in Helen face, some light coming into it we have never seen there; some struggle in the depths behind it; and her lips tremble, trying to remember something the muscles around them once knew, till at last it finds its way out, painfully, a baby sound buried under the debris of years of dumbness.)

Helen: Wah. Wah. (And again, with great effort) Wah. Wah. (Helen plunges her hand into the dwindling water, spells into her own palm. Then she gropes frantically, Annie reaches for her hand, and Helen spells into Annie's hand.)

Annie [whispering]: Yes. (Helen spells into it again.) Yes! (Helen grabs at the handle, pumps for more water, plunges her hand into its spurt and grabs Annie's to spell it again.) Yes! Oh, my dear

The Miracle Worker WILLIAM GIBSON

6

Angels and Miracles

I KNOW THAT MY INTEREST in miracles was stimulated by my interest in angels. In both the Hebrew Scriptures and the New Testament angels figure in any number of extraordinary miracles. But I believe that angels are also part of our everyday life, that everyone has a guardian angel, and that they play an important role in the performance of ordinary miracles. As I see it, when angels intervene in our lives—to protect, to rescue, to inspire, to enrich, to guide—this is not an extraordinary miracle. It does not disturb the natural laws of the universe. Rather, it is consistent with another set of laws, supernatural laws, that have been in place since our world began and even before.

"I totally believe that God always wants the best for us, no matter what," Matt Bruce, a Columbine sophomore who belongs to a youth group a St. Frances Cabrini Church in Littleton, Colorado, was quoted as saying in a *New York Times* article on Sunday, June 6, 1999. Matt was in the cafeteria when Eric Harris and Dylan Klebold went through the school in their murderous rampage. "I feel there were thousands of angels in there protecting people, helping people."

47

On national television, one blonde-haired, handsome, athletic boy, when asked about his experiences, told this story. One of the gunmen came over to him and pointed his gun right at his head. "I closed my eyes, thought of my parents, and prayed hard, knowing I was going to die." He heard the gun go off, but when he opened his eyes, he realized that the killer, who was then going after someone else, had missed at close range. When the news commentator expressed amazement and suggested that the young man had indeed been lucky, the boy replied: "I don't think it was luck. I believe in angels. My guardian angel saved me."

But when Cassie Bernall, seventeen, was asked by one of the gunmen if she believed in God, she answered yes, and he proceeded to murder her then and there.

So where is the loving hand of God in all this? How can you speak of miracles and angels in the face of such a tragedy? Many of the youngsters who survived the Columbine shootings did not appear to have serious trouble with these questions. In fact, even though quite upset, many of them spurned the crisis intervention counselors who were sent to give them an opportunity to talk about what they had experienced, express and deal with their fear and anger, and begin to distance themselves from the awful nightmare. Instead, they went to their churches and their clergymen for guidance, in an effort to understand what had happened within a world view that included faith in a personal God and acknowledged the reality of evil. "God gathered up His army of angels and protected as many people as He could," Sara Martin, a senior who is a member of the Evangelical Presbyterian Church, is quoted as having said. "The whole school was meant to blow up. Good always overpowers evil."

One of my patients, a forty-seven year old woman, related this story to me. "Some years ago, before I met you, I was so depressed I wanted to kill myself. So I drove to a beach and took a bottle full of sleeping tablets. I thought that before I lost consciousness, I could swim out to sea and make it look like an accident. I was dead serious.

"But then, my angel spoke to me . . . I don't mean I hear voices, that's not the way he communicates . . . and told me to go to a phone booth nearby and call my husband. It was as if he was literally pushing me in that direction. I dialed the number. I felt groggier and groggier, listening to the ring. I counted them, one, two, three . . . waiting for the answering machine to pick up. He couldn't be home at this hour. I knew that. I was only doing what my angel demanded of me.

"Then, I heard my husband's voice. I could hardly speak now. I told him I was at a beach and had taken pills and was going to die. I told him I loved him and I was very sorry, but I couldn't stand the pain any longer. When he asked me exactly where I was located, I hung up. I barely got out of the booth before I collapsed in a coma.

"Now my husband is a very bright man. He called the state police right away. He told them I was at a payphone at the beach. There were only a couple of payphones there. They knew right where to go. In minutes the police and the emergency medical team were on the scene. I recall waking up in a daze as they carried me on a stretcher to the ambulance. I felt enveloped by my angel, as if he had surrounded me to protect me, and he stayed with me all the way to the hospital.

"My doctor later said that contacting my husband was a cry for help. I know it wasn't. I wanted to die. It was my angel who stopped me in my tracks. And now that I am so much better, I am eternally grateful to him."

I asked her what she had taken away from that experience.

"A new appreciation of life," she quickly answered. "I know God wants me to live. Until then, I had been floundering for years. Of course, I hadn't been well physically. I have severe arthritis and fibromyalgia that causes me a lot of pain most of the time. But I have courage. I've rededicated myself to my husband and family, and I'm starting to take part in a community program to help disabled children. It's like being born all over again. And I have my angel to thank for that."

When a friend of mine told me of the following experience, it seemed to me a very ordinary miracle had taken place. Let's call him George. He had stopped by to visit an acquaintance one Saturday afternoon He rang the front door bell. No one answered. He walked back to his car, but as he was opening the door, he felt a powerful urge to walk around to the back of the house, where he saw a two year old child perched precariously on the edge of a swimming pool. There was no adult in sight. He ran desperately to the little boy and snatched him up in his arms even as he was about to plunge into the water. Then, turning around, he saw a teen-age girl emerging through French doors onto to the terrace, a look of pure fear etched on her face. "I went in just for a second to answer the phone," she said, pleadingly. "He was right here on the terrace. I don't know how he could have gotten so far so fast. Thank God you were here!"

"I used to think what I felt was ESP. But now I'm sure I was being prodded by an angel," George said.

Rev. Benedict J. Groeschel tells of a Brother Brendan Lague, O.F.M., a missionary in China at the time of the Japanese occupation.

On May 14, 1943, the Japanese army entered the walled city of Shasi, province of Hupeh, from one direction while the friars escaped through the gate on the opposite side of the city. Escape was necessary because they had been told that the army would kill all foreigners they found. Brother Brendan was quite young, but he lagged behind taking care of an elderly friar. When they arrived at the top of an adjoining hill and saw the path divide, they did not know which way their companions had gone. They were preparing to go to the right when a figure of a man was suddenly in front of them. He said, "No, go to the left." . . . [The man] was clothed in ordinary Chinese attire but was not oriental. Brother Brendan could not remember whether he heard the man speak in English or Chinese, but for the moment he felt certain that this non-Oriental person standing there in the midst of the Chinese countryside looked like Saint Joseph. They followed his instructions. As they ran down the path to the left, they could hear machine gun fire right behind them toward the path to the right. Had they gone to the right they would have been killed immediately.

Joan Webster Anderson, in her book *Where Miracles Happen*, devotes a section to ordinary miracles in which angels seem to have played central roles. For example, she tells a story about a woman named Emilie, who had become pregnant, even though she was nearly forty years old and had previously had surgery that made pregnancy almost impossible. Driving home after a visit to her obstetrician, she was caught in a blizzard. Her car became stuck in ice and snow on a deserted road. Terrified, she began to pray. She also considered her options. She could climb a steep hill in front of her in search of help. She could try to dig herself out. But either way, she would be seriously risking her pregnancy.

Suddenly she saw a tall man making his way toward her through the snow. A station wagon was parked behind him. Going behind her car, he pushed it until it started. Emilie guided it easily up the hill, in spite of deepening snow drifts. When she reached the top, neither the man nor his station wagon were in sight.

Many of the stories in Anderson's book connect angels with ordinary miracles. A man falls over the side of his sail boat. He prays. When he is found, an hour later, he is too weak to hold onto the rope that's thrown him. He feels strong hands, supporting him, helping him. But when he is aboard the boat again, no one is visible in the water.

The lights of a mysterious truck save a nurse on her way home from being assaulted by three thugs. At a baseball game, a father hears a voice in his head telling him that his four-year-old daughter will be struck in the head by a ball that would be hit into the bleachers, if he doesn't do something to protect her. Suddenly a player does hit a long, hard ball. Already alerted, her father quickly raises his arm as a shield, and it strikes him instead of his little girl.

The town official at Lourdes (played by Vincent Price, remember?) on hearing accounts like these, would probably smile cynically and remark at how gullible people can be. Many psychiatrists would probably regard hearing voices of angels in your head or seeing them point the way to safety as hallucinations, and consult their diagnostic manual to see where you might fit in. At best, they would regard your attitude as a childish and magical interpretation of reality, to be corrected in the course of psychoanalytic therapy.

But not all psychiatrists. At a recent meeting of the American Psychiatric Association, a psychiatrist who had seen my book about angels took me aside and told me that, the previous year, he had had to go to the hospital for major surgery. He asked his sister to pray for him. She said she would do so in a prayer group at her church, and that she would *ask an angel to hold him tight and look after him.*

"The night before surgery I was lying in my bed. I hadn't been medicated yet. I thought I'd get up and walk around. But something forcibly held me there. I felt a warm and tingling sensation, and I thought of what my sister had promised, and believe you me, I was utterly astonished. I survived the surgery extraordinarily well."

A 1989 Gallup poll reported that 83% of Americans believe in miracles. That's about the same number who claim to believe in angels, and in God, and who feel that God plays a providential role in their lives, if they allow Him to, and that, one way or another, He hears and responds to their prayers.

7

Providence

IN ORDER TO UNDERSTAND the difference between extraordinary miracles and ordinary ones, we must clearly distinguish between the impossible and the improbable. It is impossible for the dead to rise again, but Elijah and Jesus both brought the dead back to life, and Jesus was resurrected Himself, three days after His crucifixion. It was impossible for Naaman to be cured instantaneously of his leprosy by washing seven times in the river Jordan as he was told to do by Elisha, but he was. Nor was it possible for anyone to walk on water, as Jesus did, or for the sun to shake and spin and rush down toward 50,000 onlookers as it did at Fatima, or for Juan Diego's cloak, hanging in the basilica on Tepayac Hill in Mexico City, to still bear a full-length image of Christ's mother. It would appear impossible that 20-year-old Jeanne Tulasne, suffering with advanced Pott's disease—tuberculosis having caused the destruction of two or three vertebrae, with marked curvature of the dorsolumbar spine, a bone abscess in the left thigh, muscular atrophy and clubfoot—was cured suddenly and lastingly at Lourdes on September 8, 1897.

Ordinary miracles are improbable happenings. It would strike most of us as highly improbable that fifteen people, scheduled to meet at a certain accessible place and convenient and customary time, would all be late. But that's precisely what took place in an event described by Richard Blodgett in *Readers Digest* in September, 1987. Referring to an article that originally appeared in *Life* magazine, Blodgett tells of fifteen people scheduled to attend a rehearsal of a church choir in Beatrice, Nebraska, on March 1, 1950. All were late, each for a different reason — 'a car wouldn't start, a program one was listening to on the radio hadn't ended yet, ironing wasn't finished, a conversation dragged on.' But not one of them showed up at the agreed upon time, 7:15 P.M. The church was destroyed by an explosion at 7:25. The odds of all fifteen being late the same evening were calculated to be one-in-a-million.

BEYOND SYNCHRONICITY

I've always been interested in Carl Jung's concept of synchronicity. According to Jung, seemingly accidental occurrences in our lives may actually be somehow connected with one another, in some inexplicable fashion. He described this as the simultaneous occurrence of two meaningfully but not causally connected events, 'equal in rank to causality as a principle of explanation.' He emphasized that *meaningfulness* is what differentiates synchronicity from plain coincidence.

Over the years, I've often considered this process when I observed a special coming together of events, especially beneficial ones, as if designed and driven by some mysterious influence. For example, one of my early patients, a twenty-eight-year-old woman named Charlotte, consulted me for depression. She had had several very disappointing and demoralizing relationships with men over the years. Once we had worked out her hurts and resentments and put her on the right path again—it took nearly two years of therapy to accomplish this—she expressed some dismay over the fact that "now that I'm ready for a real relationship, my chances of finding someone seem so remote."

A few months after completing therapy, she received a letter from a former college teacher with whom she had been friends. He was ten years older than she, and although they were clearly attracted to one another, they respected the ethical considerations of the teacher-student relationship, and her youthfulness in particular. He married someone else. But in the letter he told her that his wife had died and left him with two small children. He wondered if they might meet, for old times' sake. They did. They fell in love, married, and now have children of their own.

This only served to strengthen my conviction that Jung had been onto something.

But what?

Jung had no explanation for what he had observed, not even a reasonable speculation, only that something was going on beyond any one individual's spatial confines. It was only a more careful look at Jung's writings in recent years that made me realize that I had extended upon the parameters of his notions about synchronicity. He had actually delineated three types of the phenomenon. First, there might be a coincidence between a thought and a simultaneous outer event. This is a very common occurrence. You think of your friend Cynthia whom you haven't heard from in months, and lo and behold, the telephone rings, and there is she is, on the other end of the line. This is often viewed as an example of extra-sensory perception, or ESP.

The second form of synchronicity is seen when you have a dream or a vision that coincides with an event that occurs at the same moment in time some distance away. My mother, waking up with a sense of dread, fearing that something had happened to me the night I spent in a capsized boat drifting in a current along the Cuban coast, could qualify for this. Again, a form of ESP?

The third form is prophetic. You have a premonition, a vision, or a dream, about something that may happen in the future, and indeed, the event does take place. Again, most of us are familiar with such experiences. One of my daughters, three-thousand miles away, sensed something was wrong with my health, months before my prostate cancer was discovered. Is this the kind of intuitive communication that can occur between people who have been very close for many years? I recall a dream of my own, when I was fourteen years old. In it, I'd returned to school after the Christmas holidays, only to find out, to my horror, that the exams scheduled for the end of January were going to be given the next day. I wasn't prepared. Usually a good student, I did poorly and felt humiliated. In fact, the tests were given as originally planned. I thought I had done enough studying for them. But in spite of that, I drew down a C+, in contrast to my usual A.

Without realizing it, I had invented a fourth form of synchronicity, seemingly coincidental events coming together to significantly influence a person's future life, as in Charlotte's case. You miss the 7:02 morning commuter train, so you take the 7:46. You're fuming about being late to work. But sitting next to you is the owner of a company in the same kind of business you're in. By the time you reach the city, he's asked you to send him your resume and set up an appointment to see him. You haven't been that happy where you are, so you do. And you end up being offered a better job at better pay with someone you really can respect.

I don't know why it took so long for it to dawn on me that Jung's ideas about synchronicity—or perhaps, to be more accurate, my innocent extension of his concept—closely resembled a phenomenon with which we have been familiar since the time of Joseph being sold into slavery in Egypt, if not before: Providence, the hand of God acting in our lives.

As soon as you begin to think about remarkable events in your life, things that seem to have occurred by mere chance, in a different light, the reality of ordinary miracles becomes apparent.

A good friend of mine, call her Lisa, a woman in her fifties, attends services several times a month at her local Baptist church. Several years ago, she was diagnosed as having breast cancer. At a healing service, she told her minister about it, mentioning that she had been trying to get an appointment in the near future with a well-known doctor in the field, but that she had not been able to succeed. "Why, that's my doctor," her minister said. "I have an appointment with him next week. You can take my slot."

After examining her, the surgeon recommended a radical mastectomy, the removal of her entire breast and all lymph nodes in the area. Lisa told him that was not what she wanted and asked him to refer her to someone for a second opinion. She then gave him the list of doctors participating in her health plan. He recognized one surgeon's name and recommended her without reservation, referring to her humorously, but with respect, as a "breast conservationist." Lisa had a lumpectomy and chemotherapy and appears to be doing just fine. She also told me that her minister was part of a nationwide prayer network and that she was included in their petitions.

My Personal Encounters with Providence

I don't have to look any further than my own life to find evidence of providential miracles. When I applied to medical school in my last year of college, I asked my favorite teacher, Father Gerard Murphy, a Jesuit professor of social studies, for a letter of recommendation. He agreed, suggesting that I give serious consideration to specializing in psychiatry. I had only the vaguest notion of what psychiatry was at the time. Having served in the Navy during the war, I knew that during the enlistment process I was interviewed by a psychiatrist whose only question I recall was about what I did in my spare time. I also knew that a 'section eight discharge' meant you were being separated from the service because you were mentally unbalanced.

During my years at the New York Hospital-Cornell University Medical College, I kept Father Murphy's words in mind, but I was more attracted to the field of neurosurgery. I spent three months as a substitute intern, making rounds with Dr. Bronson Ray, an eminent neurosurgeon, and holding retractors for him during his operative procedures. When it was over, Dr. Ray told me that neurosurgery was already an overcrowded field, which it really wasn't, and that he too thought I should become a psychiatrist.

I wasn't too happy about this suggestion. I had very mixed feelings about psychiatry in those days. Except for Alec Guiness as the psychiatrist in T. S. Eliot's play, *The Cocktail Party*, and Ingrid Bergman in Alfred Hitchcock's *Spellbound*, and Leo Genn in *The Snake Pit*, the first-hand images I had of psychiatrists were not especially flattering. With a few exceptions, they seemed to be a breed apart from the rest of my physician colleagues—not very sociable and seeming at times as much in need of therapy as their patients. My classmates and teachers also discouraged me from choosing the field. My parents weren't exactly very thrilled with the idea either.

So when I completed my internship in medicine at Bellevue Hospital in New York, I was very confused as to where to go next in my career. Most of us interns there were barely recovering from our own brand of acute traumatic stress disorder. Twenty-four years old, we had been continually faced with managing life-or-death crises. Forty-eight hours on duty with practically no sleep, then twelve hours off, and back again to the nightmarish ordeal.

I thought that preventive medicine might offer an interesting career path, and I began studies at the School of Public Health and Administrative Medicine at the Columbia School of Physicians and Surgeons in New York. Within four months I realized that I'd made the wrong choice. I felt quite uncertain about my future, so I consulted a psychologist who specialized in career counseling. He gave me a lot of tests and told me my talents and skills were very suited to psychiatry. At that point, telling me that I would be well suited for anything was enough to lift my spirits.

Looking for spiritual guidance, I made a three day retreat in prayer at a Jesuit facility, St. Andrew's on the Hudson, in Poughkeepsie, New York. When I returned to the city, I made an appointment to see Dr. Oskar Diethelm, the head of the department of psychiatry at the Payne Whitney Clinic of the New York Hospital. It was February. I asked him to accept me for the residency training program starting in July, concerned that once he realized how conflicted I was about being a psychiatrist, he would reject me out of hand. I also had in hand a letter of recommendation from another one of my mentors, the chairman of the department of medicine, who added to my distress by telling me that he was sorry about my decision, since, as he saw it, I would have made a fine doctor. To my surprise, Dr. Diethelm told me he'd be pleased to have me on the staff and, that, since he had a vacancy, he wanted me to start my training immediately.

Looking back over the years, I'm convinced that psychiatry has truly been the right vocation for me. And it seems as if every time I tried to avoid getting into it, coincidences would conspire to channel me back in that direction. I used to regard this as an example of synchronicity. I now recognize it as one of providence.

I dare say that not every coincidental happening reflects divine involvement, unless one accurately believes that God is a player in everything that occurs in one's life. I think that the idea of divine providence should be reserved for those seemingly random events that truly make a difference, like the time that my own physician did a prostate specific antigen level (or PSA, a test to determine activity of the prostate gland, in which elevated levels suggest the possibility of prostate inflammation or malignancy). It was done in March, as part of a full battery of routine tests: white and red blood counts, cholesterol, hemoglobin, sugar. My report came back "fine," but I failed to notice that the PSA report was not specifically noted. In July of the same year, the New York Hospital (now called New York Presbyterian Hospital), where I was and am an attending psychiatrist, requested a statement from my doctor as part of the usual biannual reappointment to the staff. I sent the form off to him to complete. A few days later he phoned me. He admitted, apologetically, but very honestly, that the report had been originally misfiled and that when he looked in my records to prepare his summary, he had found it there. And the PSA was clearly elevated. He recommended a biopsy of the prostate, which I had done within a few days and which unfortunately revealed a malignant tumor. I proceeded to have surgery. There were no metastases. Eight years later, I seem to be in excellent health.

A few of my friends felt that the misfiling of the test results was outrageous and unforgivable. But I look at the matter quite differently. I was angry at first, sure, but I came to terms with it and forgave a mistake that could have happened to anyone. My doctor is an excellent, honest doctor. He always practices cutting-edge medicine; the PSA test was not in general use at the time he drew my blood for it. It would have been a simple matter to cover up his secretary's error. But he didn't. As soon as he discovered it, he contacted me personally so that we could proceed with the evaluation.

I consider this an act of God's providence, that my doctor did the test at all, and that the report was found when the hospital requested an update on my health. Without that, another year might have elapsed and the tumor, an aggressive one, might have spread beyond the capsule of the prostate and I might be in serious difficulty today, if not dead. I also consider it providential that one of the country's leading prostate cancer surgeons was the head of the urology department at my own hospital and known personally to me, and it was he to whom I turned for help.

Another example of providence operating in my life involved my daughter Rickie. In 1966, when I was thirty-nine years old, my eldest daughter, Rickie, was hospitalized for what my colleagues thought to be a schizophrenic illness. She was thirteen years old. Over the next nine years she was in and out of hospitals, unsuccessfully treated as if she were schizophrenic when, in fact, she had been suffering with an affective disorder, a depression and a serious visual perceptual impairment (which may have been a precursor of the condition from which she now suffers, Ehlers Danloff syndrome). In desperation, I turned to the only place I could for help for Rickie. I prayed. I prayed a lot. I prayed especially for the intercession of St. Jude. I asked her to pray too, although I didn't have to. It was something she always did.

Suddenly, in 1974, when everything seemed quite hopeless, our prayers were heard. A series of providential happenings. I had just published a new book about depression. A film producer, Norman Weissman, driving to New York along the Connecticut Turnpike, heard its first chapter read on the radio. He bought the book, read it, and phoned me to get together one day for lunch. I didn't talk about Rickie much in those days. It was too painful. But I felt an immediate trust and connectedness with Norman, and did so. He asked me if I'd ever had her vision checked. His question seemed to come out of left field. "I've been doing a documentary about work going on at the Gissell Institute in New Haven," he explained. "Children with autism and other kinds of psychiatric illnesses have been shown to have visual perceptual disorders, and when these are corrected, many of their emotional and behavioral symptoms improve."

As a consequence of Norman's enthusiasm and urging, I had Rickie's vision evaluated by a specialist in visual perception. Indeed, she did have a serious form of blindness affecting the brain centers of her vision, erratic, clearing up at times, made worse by stress, definitely not of hysterical origin, and to some degree reversible with proper treatment. I arranged for her to be treated for her condition. I also removed her from the care of my psychiatric colleagues, transferred her to a rehabilitation program (quite pioneering in those days and professionally scoffed at), where she could learn how to function in the world again. Over the next six months, Rickie experienced a remarkable recovery.

I have always looked at Rickie's improvement as the answer to prayer. The entire train of events, from my first meeting with Norman to helping Rickie find an apartment when it was time for her to go out on her own, was filled with so many inexplicable happenings that I cannot fail to see God's hand in it. A miracle? Not one that defied the laws of nature, but a providential miracle, one that can and does happen to most of us more than once in our lifetimes, one that may require the soil of faith for it to take place.

PROVIDENCE IN THE LIVES OF MY PATIENTS

I see numerous examples of meaningful coincidence in the lives of my patients. This past year, a forty-year-old woman—call her Rebecca—consulted me because she had happened to catch me on a television interview program. She seldom watches television. She telephoned me to find out if I still saw patients. A few, I replied. She made an appointment. I discovered that she had been seeing a psychotherapist for several years. She had also been given antidepressants by a psychopharmacologist. But her feelings of futility, difficulty concentrating, persistent lateness, inability to move forward with her life continued to plague her. By the third visit, I had gathered enough evidence to suggest a diagnosis of Attention Deficit Disorder. She was astonished. By our next visit, she had already read half a dozen books and searched the internet to find out whatever she could on the subject , and was convinced that she had been suffering with ADD since childhood. The diagnosis had never before been made in her case.

But she refused to take any of the medications, such as methylphenidate (Ritalin) commonly used to treat her condition. So I recommended that she consult a developmental optometrist, to determine whether she also had a visual perceptual disability that might lend itself to correction. I am probably one of the few psychiatrists in New York who would even think of such an option because of my previous experiences with visual perceptual disability. She made the appointment without further delay. Indeed she had such a problem. Within two months of starting visual training, she noticed a substantial improvement in her ability to function in just about every aspect of her life and her depression largely subsided.

There are several important points that are illustrated in both my own case and that of my patient's. When my physician called to tell me of my PSA finding and when Rebecca saw me on television, neither of us were forced to do anything about it. Not do anything about it, when your PSA is elevated as mine was, you may ask? Believe me, a great many people ignore dangers to their health, even when these are staring them in the face. And many people, getting nowhere in their efforts to get well, could dream up a dozen reasons not to reach out to a new professional or a new possibility for help, even when a feeling of hope had been ignited.

The choice is always ours. God gave us the right and responsibility to exercise free will.

Jean Tulasne did not have to go to Lourdes. Charlotte didn't have to answer the letter of her former teacher. I could have ignored all the signposts that directed me toward becoming a psychiatrist, and specialized in cardiology or internal medicine instead. Lisa was not forced to attend the healing service at her church, nor was she compelled to accept the appointment with the specialist her pastor offered her. I could have denied the potential dangers associated with my prostate condition and postponed treatment until it could have been too late, as many men, highly intelligent ones, have done. Had I not acted by removing Rickie from the care of the psychiatrists who were then treating her and followed up on the leads that Norman had given me, she might still be lingering in mental institutions instead of being married, the mother of three children, and a nurse.

When providential events take place—and again, by these I mean a series of coincidences that offer a chance to profoundly affect the course of our lives—it is paramount that we be able to recognize what is happening and cooperate with them as best we can. The litmus test for their divine origin is where the journeys take us. Inevitably they will take us closer to God's will, to find new strength, the fulfillment of our personal gifts and talents, greater harmony and generosity in our relationships with others, a deeper knowledge of loving, a deeper sense of God Himself. And if we've read the signals incorrectly, or ultimately find no special significance to them, we can simply acknowledge the fact and go on about our business until we discover the true direction we are meant to take.

PART IV

Healing
and
Prayer

Mother, sing me a song
That will ease my pain
Mend my broken bones,
Bring wholeness again.

Catch my babies
When they are born
Sing my death song,
Teach me how to mourn.

Show me the Medicine
Of the healing herbs,
The value of spirit,
The way I can serve.

Mother, heal my heart
So that I can see
The gifts of yours
That can live through me.

NATIVE AMERICAN PRAYER FOR HEALING

8

Healing the Mind

SINCE I AM A PSYCHIATRIST, most of the miraculous healings that I have witnessed have to do largely with the psyche, and with human relationships. Here again, I use the word 'miracle' not to describe something that involves an exception to the natural order of things, but rather something that is highly improbable.

A MIRACULOUS RECONCILIATION

Harold was sixty years old when he first came to see me several years ago. He not only presented a picture of a very anxious man, but a very unhappy one too. He was a person of wonderful values. On Friday evenings, he regularly attended services at his local synagogue, remembering his long dead parents in his prayers, and praying for health and contentment for himself and his family. He was financially comfortable, owned his own home, and was well respected in his work as owner of a small chain of menswear stores.

But Harold and his wife Bernice had been emotionally estranged for years, although they still lived together and went through the motions of being a married couple and parents to their three grown children. Their oldest son was an electrical engineer, who seemed to be very successful in his career and happily married with two children. Their next son was a source of constant worry. He had been floundering for years, holding down a job at an automobile dealership that held little future and made no demands on his exceptional abilities, apparently unmotivated to find any other kind of work.

My first task was to help alleviate Harold's anxiety and encourage him to adopt a more optimistic attitude toward his life. This effort required a long period of psychotherapy, two years in fact, during which time we worked on everything from childhood fears to serious regret at not having gone to college, to disappointment and self-criticism over a business career that had been very mediocre until the last ten years, to unresolved grief over his father's death six years before (since which time his anxiety had grown a good deal worse), to controlling a nasty temper and cultivating more patience in general, to improving his relationship with his wife, and finally, to starting him on one of the newer antidepressants, which he tolerated well and to which he responded very satisfactorily with less anxiety, fewer angry outbursts, and less of a pessimistic outlook.

From time to time, I asked whether he thought Bernice would come to see me too. He was convinced she wouldn't. He did suggest it a few times, but each time she declined.

Then, one day, she called me and asked to see me. An explosive argument between them had made her think of separation and divorce.

Bernice proved to be a lovely woman, generous to a fault, who had stifled her own angry feelings for years, hoping against hope that her relationship with Harold would improve, but finally resigning herself to an empty marriage, turning to her children and her successful career as an interior decorator as her sources of fulfillment.

She agreed to postpone her decision and to meet with her husband and me together.

Ordinarily, when I see a couple who have had difficulties for years,

I hardly expect much to be accomplished without a very long period of hard work in therapy, if at all. In fact, it took only six one-and-a-half hour visits with me for the two of them to put years of misunderstandings into words, forgive each other for all the hurts and misunderstandings, learn something about how each one really thought and felt about many things for the very first time, and come together with a sense of joy, affection, and renewed commitment. "We haven't felt this way toward each other since we were first in love," they both affirmed.

Six months later, Harold, who still drops in to see me now from time to time for a kind of refresher, informed me that his younger son seemed to have "miraculously" come alive—Harold's word, not mine—and that he had gone out and located a terrific new job in the burgeoning world of telecommunications.

I can't explain the remarkable resurrection of this man's life entirely from a medical vantage point. I did everything by the book. But while the odds of his own, individual improvement were pretty good with therapy, all the rest that happened and the speed with which it took place runs counter to my forty years of practice. Not an impossible outcome, but certainly a very unlikely one. An answer to prayer? Harold prayed regularly. I pray for my patients every day, a short, silent prayer asking God to guide me in my work and aid in their recovery. And our prayers were undoubtedly helped by the fact that both Harold and Bernice were honest, well-meaning people, motivated to do the very best with their lives and imbued with the principle of wishing all others well.

SPIRITUALITY AND PSYCHIATRIC TREATMENT

According to Dr. Francis MacNutt, in his book *Healing*, faith in God's power to heal may rest in the person praying for healing, the sick or troubled person asking for help, or even "when no one in particular seems to have faith," when God just wants to manifest His goodness. When I first read MacNutt's comment, I found it perplexing. A former Dominican priest whose life's work is healing through prayer, he seemed to have covered all bases. But giving it more thought, I realize that this is probably true.

In the first place, few people are probably without any faith in God, although they may not explicitly believe in God's intervention in the healing process. And, since I am recounting my own clinical experiences, I would qualify as a professional who prays that my work with patients be effective, privately, every day. But no less remarkable outcomes are achieved by a number of my colleagues in the mental health field who are agnostics, that is, who feel they have no way of knowing whether a personal God exists and that they must rely on their own skills and judgment to help their patients get well.

After all, the true agnostic approaches the question of God's existence with an open mind. Maybe there is a Divine Creator, Who also keeps things going. But, then again, maybe there isn't it. A number of people I know think this way, and the lives they lead are as driven by a goodness, a holiness, that is far superior to that I find among many of my church-going friends. In fact, there's probably a little bit of agnosticism in every believer. Except perhaps for the saints and a handful of others whose faith has never wavered, I'm sure we've all had our uncertainties at one time or another.

Whether they believe or have their doubts, good therapists employ the essential elements of spiritual healing, even if they aren't aware of doing so. They understand that every person who voluntarily comes to them arrives in a state of bewilderment, fear, futility, desperation. Many are afraid they are losing their minds, going crazy. Many believe nothing can be done for them. Many have been through horrific experiences, from abuse during childhood, to divorce, the death of a child, or professional and financial disaster. They are utterly demoralized.

As the eminent psychiatrist Jerome Frank pointed out, restoring a patient's morale is the first step in helping him or her overcome feelings of helplessness and confusion and beginning to understand what's been happening. In listening to the story, the therapist is learning not only what has been going on, within the person and within his or her life, but also attempting to picture how the person is experiencing what he or she is experiencing. The goal is to help the patient both make sense out of it and regain some command of his or her life.

This is often done by offering a medical explanation for the patient's distress, for example, by saying, when it's appropriate, something like "What you're experiencing is what we doctors call a depression." But it's no less important to reassure the patient that, in all likelihood, being depressed isn't the basic disorder—since depression, for most people, still connotes weakness or a form of mental illness—but rather it is the patient's inability to understand and deal with his or her condition and recover from it spontaneously, without the need for professional intervention. This is also accomplished by helping the individual see connections between his or her current emotional distress and life events that have contributed to this, events he or she may have forgotten, overlooked, or underestimated as to their significance.

Then, the effective therapist, in the course of assessing a patient's strengths, coping skills, and the availability of supportive people in his or her environment, will also try to determine where a philosophy of life, spirituality, and faith (or lack thereof) about a personal God or a divine force for good in the universe fit in.

Now this could be particularly difficult for therapists who are wedded to a very mechanistic, materialistic, essentially atheistic view of human nature, such as that offered by Freud. That is probably why so few of them inquire about their patients' religious lives. It may also explain, in part, for the high number of therapeutic failures with which we are all too familiar. Naturally, one must also take the talent, skill, and experience of the therapist into account, as well as the fact that a number of patients suffering with psychiatric disorders are as intractable to present-day treatments as are many cases of cancer.

Being a psychiatrist, people seldom come to see me because they are experiencing their distress as spiritual in nature. My inquiry into their religious beliefs is often cursory at first, but I stay alert to learning more about these as therapy progresses, with special attention to whether their emotional crisis is also a spiritual one. I do feel it's my responsibility as their doctor to understand how they perceive their lives, and in particular the pain and confusion that brought them to me. At the very least, I must relieve any embarrassment or humiliation they may feel at having fallen apart emotionally or being as incapacitated as they find themselves, and this I can do only if I can grasp what their "illness" means to them.

But beyond that, understanding their belief systems has important implications for treatment. Years ago, psychiatrists Frederick Redlich and August Hollingshead observed that when patients and their therapists shared similar values and background experience, the therapeutic outcome was significantly better than when they did not. This can be quite a dilemma for millions of religious people seeking help from mental health professionals, the majority of whom are not religious. Fortunately, really good therapists are able to work within their patients' world-view, without having to seriously compromise their own. "Suspended judgment, sensitivity, and genuine interest must be the hallmarks of requestioning that touches upon closely held values and beliefs," wrote psychiatrist Irving S. Wiesner. Wiesner suggests that therapists ask such questions as: Do you come from a particular religious, spiritual, or philosophical background? Do you adhere to any particular belief or faith system? How important is this to your everyday life, and how does this belief system and your application of it affect your present problems?

"Under the stress of their psychiatric difficulties, some patients demonstrate regression in their beliefs and values," he wrote. "They are confused and disappointed that their world view has failed to protect or adequately explain their current situation . . . Patients, in any case, are challenged to test the 'sea worthiness' of their beliefs."

Wiesner cites the case of a twenty-five-year-old recently married woman who consulted him for depression, who found herself in both emotional and spiritual turmoil. Her mother was seriously ill and not expected to live. For the prior three years, the mother had not spoken to her daughter because she (the patient) had left the religious group in which she was raised and then married a man from another denomination of the same religion. She still maintained a deep faith that reflected the basic tenets of her parents' religious group, but she had moved away from their rigidity and authoritarianism. The daughter now felt a great sense of guilt for her 'disloyalty' that was markedly exasperated by her mother's impending death.

"Her anger toward her mother for her (the mother's) lack of nurturance," Wiesner described, "is validated by the therapist [Wiesner], who also helps her work through the process of forgiveness—a very important principle in her world view. She is able to move toward accepting her mother's limitations and reach out to her in spite of them."

He adds that consultation with the patient's pastor enabled him to better understand the context of the patient's struggles, and "this, in turn, facilitates healing."

BELIEF SYSTEMS AND MENTAL ABERRATIONS

We doctors must also be alert to ways in which patients' belief systems can get all tied up with their psychopathology. Consider the nature of belief systems. They're universal social phenomena that constitute a significant and central aspect of any culture. They're important for maintaining the organization and vitality of the group, as well as for young people growing up in the society who eventually will share in its culture. The contents of belief systems vary as do their context. They may be political or scientific. Most often they involve religious or philosophical thinking, to help people understand aspects of reality in terms of coherent explanations that are not supported scientifically at all points by explicit evidence.

Even as they may be extremely important to help guide us through life, one's beliefs may also become a vehicle for the expression of neurotic or psychotic elements in a patient's illness. "On this level, the focus falls on the pathological systems it operates in the patient's personality," wrote Dr. W. W. Meissner, "bypassing the question of pathological components embedded within the belief system itself. If the patients are caught up, for example, in endless self-accusations and tormented convictions that because of their sinfulness they are condemned to an eternity of damnation in hell, their scrupulosity would not necessarily persuade us that there was anything pathological about the religious beliefs they embraced. We would be more likely to think that the pathology resided in the neurotic use to which they put the belief system."

Belief systems themselves can become pathological. Meissner continues: "To the extent that a patient's religious belief system involves content or principles that prevent or subvert effective and adaptive functioning or contribute to personality disturbances or symptomatic disruptions, we would judge that system [itself] to be psychiatrically pathological." He points out that certain cults can be identified as pathological systems, a result of the forces that contribute to their formation, such as rebelliousness, or the messianic and mesmerizing power of their leaders over their naive and misguided followers, searching for a way to cope with their sense of helplessness, in search of meaning.

Freud considered all religious faith to be a form of mass delusion, and therefore to be regarded as pathological. But this is not what psychiatrists have in mind by the term delusion. In a standard psychiatric dictionary, delusion is defined as "a belief engendered without appropriate external stimulation and maintained by one in spite of what to normal beings constitutes incontrovertible and 'plain as day' proof or evidence to the contrary . . . .further, the belief held is not one which is ordinarily accepted by other members of the patient's culture or subculture."

Another definition of delusion is that it is a "false belief that is firmly maintained even though it is contradicted by social reality. While it is true that some superstitions and religious beliefs are held despite the lack of confirmatory evidence, such culturally engendered concepts are not considered delusions. What is characteristic of the delusion is that it is not shared by others . . . a thinking disorder of enough import to interfere with the subject's functioning."

There is a world of difference between radically diverse and incompatible belief systems in a pluralistic society such as the United States—from secular humanists to evangelists to freedom-of-choice and pro-life groups—and the pathological shared beliefs of groups like the Temple of God cult that extinguished itself so gruesomely at Jonestown, Guyana.

RAYMOND'S PRISON

I've occasionally encountered patients in whom religious beliefs were an integral part of their illnesses. I recall seeing a young man named Raymond for several visits in consultation. Brought up in a strict and severe fundamentalist home in New Jersey, where even dancing and card playing were considered sinful, he abided by his family's expectations until he reached his early thirties, all through college, and even during a two-year stint in the army during the Korean War. He moved to New York, intending to continue his education and obtain a master's degree in education. Half way through his first semester at Columbia University, he began to have frequent nightmares of dying and being eternally damned to the fires of hell. Up until then, he had been celibate, but his previously suppressed sexual instincts began to press in on him. He felt enormous guilt about these. On one occasion, he engaged in mild sexual petting with a young woman with whom he had become friends in school. It was his first such encounter. He was sleepless all night, gripped by overwhelming fear that he would soon die and that his nightmarish prophecies would come true. Unable to attend class, he remained in his room for several days, deeply depressed, not eating, not bathing, totally withdrawn. During this period, his mother, worried that she had not heard from him, telephoned. As the patient related the conversation to me it was apparent that his mother recognized that he was seriously disturbed and advised him to pray harder. An innocent enough suggestion, but one that fell on deaf ears, for Raymond felt himself to be hopeless and could muster neither the faith nor energy to do so.

When Raymond's advisor, concerned by his absences, came to his room and discovered the young man's condition, he insisted that he see a psychiatrist at once, and referred him to me. The young man's own reluctance to come was compounded by another phone call with his mother who insisted that he should turn to a minister of his faith for help and avoid psychiatry at all costs. It was only when his advisor made clear that he would be dismissed from the program if he failed to seek professional help that Raymond agreed to see me.

I had a hard time getting the usual medical history from the extremely tense young man who sat across from me, his eyes downcast, avoiding mine, his face without emotion, his body stiff and motionless, hands clenched tightly together in his lap. I knew guilt when I saw it, and this was guilt, overwhelming guilt, with all the fear and helplessness that goes with it.

Slowly but surely I was able to eke out his story from him, all the while trying to communicate feelings of acceptance and empathy. Here was a man whose religious convictions, instead of being a source of strength and hope, were only adding to his suffering, blinding him to any insight into his psychological state and the many nonreligious issues that were also contributing to his condition.

"There's nothing you can do," he said flatly. "I'm doomed to hell."

I knew enough about him by now to speak directly about God. "The God you believe in . . . .I thought that He was a forgiving God," I said softly.

"Yes," he replied. "But some sins are beyond forgiveness."

"I find that hard to believe."

"Believe it!" he said angrily. "You better believe it!"

"Forgive me if I don't agree."

Raymond fell silent. A minute later he said determinedly, "I want to get this over with. I'm going to get in my car and drive upstate to a forest and lose myself there and just wander around until I die."

I realized I would have to hospitalize him for his own protection, until we could find a way to alleviate his profound despair. I made the suggestion.

"Forget it!" he said.

"Then I'll have to speak with your family, Raymond. Do I have your permission to speak with them?"

"I don't care. Go ahead. But I'm not going to any hospital."

Then and there I called his parents, both of whom happened to be home. They took my call on separate extensions.

"Under no circumstances are you going to put my son in one of those asylums!" his mother said adamantly. His father, sounding subdued, said, "That's right, mother. We want him to come home."

I was faced with a dilemma. Did I involuntarily commit Raymond to Bellevue, which, if I could find another physician to agree, I could legally do? It would have been extremely difficult, since he had not made any actual suicide attempts and he could deny that he had ever mentioned suicide to me. I opted for telling the parents, who lived only an hour and a half away, that they would have to come immediately to my office and take Raymond home, if that's what they wanted, even though it was seriously against my advice.

When our appointment time was over, Raymond sat compliantly in my waiting room under the watchful eyes of my secretary. Mother and father showed up two hours later. I interrupted my session with another patient to go out to speak with them, reiterating my recommendation and telling them why.

"We can take care of our own," his mother said tersely. And with that, the three of them left. I never saw Raymond again, but I did hear what happened to him some time later from his former advisor at Columbia. "Raymond just disappeared," he told me, "about six months ago. I telephoned him to see how he was doing. His parents weren't very friendly, I must say. Apparently he went with friends on a hunting trip in the Adirondacks. He got separated from the group. He was never seen again."

I felt this sinking feeling and a wave of sadness surged through me. Should I have been tougher, I asked myself. Should I have committed Raymond, and consequences be damned? Now *I* felt helpless, guilty. Moments of helplessness and regret about decisions, even those that seemed right at the time, are part of every physician's emotional repertoire. But accepting the limits of one's own power and forgiving oneself and learning from each such experience are essential for the effective practice of medicine.

A POWER TO HEAL

Above and beyond one's training and experience, whether a therapist believes in God or doesn't know whether to do so or not, I think that all successful therapists possess to some degree a power to heal. This is a natural power, and not to be confused with the gift of healing. "I believe that healing can and may come from God through the gift of healing and the gift of faith," wrote Billy Graham in *The Holy Spirit*. "I believe the gift of healing or miracles is one a believer has or does not have. And God gives such a gift to very few."

But he goes on to say: " . . . it [healing] also comes from Him through the use of medical means . . . . Medicine and physicians (such as Luke) are of God too."

It only makes sense to me that a number of psychiatrists and other mental health professionals possess a natural healing power that can make a tremendous difference in the quality of their treatment efforts. Some of this skill is contained in strengths that are generally acknowledged to characterize any good physician, especially empathy and agape.

EMPATHY

Empathy is the ability to truly understand what other people are experiencing and to communicate this understanding to them, compassionately, with healing words and healing silences. Few things help one develop empathy like having been there oneself. In his book *Eyes to Behold Him*, Francis MacNutt cites Michael Gaydos' description of his own healing of impaired eyesight and his consequent ability to pray for others with the same problem, when MacNutt points out the common observation that "people who have been healed of a particular ailment seem to have a special gift from that point on in ministering to people with the same problem."

I know this to be true from my personal experience. In 1950, I was in a sailing accident off the coast of Cuba. I floated in the submerged wooden shell of my boat for fourteen hours, from late afternoon until sunrise the next morning, drawn along the coast by the current and rescued by a freighter owned by the Lehigh Portland Cement company. Frightened, desperate, believing that I would drown, I spent the night praying as hard as I could. For years afterward, I suffered with episodes of tension, insomnia, anxiety and irritability, and even depression, although these were not severe enough to seriously interfere with my life and it never occurred to me to seek professional help. The diagnosis of post-traumatic stress disorder had not even been dreamt of at the time.

Years later, in 1965, my father died suddenly, my eldest daughter became seriously ill, and I suddenly found myself extremely depressed. I had to get help. I did. Thanks to psychotherapy and a drug called imipramine, a miracle drug, an antidepressant that had only recently been introduced and about which I had, in fact, carried out research studies, I not only recovered my health, but I found myself in better shape than I had ever been since my accident. It was like going back nearly twenty years and picking up the emotional pieces of my life, but with the depth and wisdom with which all I had gone through had blessed me.

From then on, when I leaned forward in my chair and said to a frightened, depressed patient, "I understand what you are going through," I did understand, and without having to spell out why in so many words, my patient invariably knew I spoke the truth and felt reassured by it.

AGAPE VS. ORDINARY HUMAN LOVE

The word "agape," from the Greek, is used to describe God's love or the love of Christ for mankind. Billy Graham explains: " When Jesus says 'love your enemies' Matthew uses the word *agape*. When Jesus says 'love one another,' John uses a*gape*. When He says 'Love they neighbor,' Mark uses *agape*. Agape is defined as 'that highest and noblest form of love which sees something infinitely precious in its object . . . It is a gift of the Holy Spirit!"

The dictionary also defines agape as meaning unselfish, platonic love of one person for another, in contrast to the more self-centered feelings and emotions associated with romantic and sexual love. Agape involves actively willing the well-being of someone else. Ordinary, human love is as often concerned with getting as with giving. It's vulnerable to shifting moods and sentiments and cannot be turned on and off at will. It is the kind of love that brings joy at times, and at other times, total despair. It can be choked out of existence by resentment and nullified by selfish desires.

Medical ethicists strongly caution doctors not to become emotionally involved with patients under their care. Common sense delivers the same message, especially for healers of the mind. Not only might such feelings lead to complicated entanglements, but they can seriously distort a therapist's perception of what is taking place in treatment and interfere with a patient's ability to recover.

But this does not mean the physician should be without feeling. This is humanly impossible. Part of psychiatrists' training is to prepare them to recognize and then correctly manage whatever feelings are aroused within them in their relationships with patients. Such emotional responses can even be used for intelligent therapeutic purposes, as when a patient unknowingly triggers a therapist's anger or is sexually enticing when, in fact, he or she is only unconsciously searching for compassion and understanding.

There is a general consensus, and research studies confirm this, that love is a powerful ingredient in all healing, even human love if it is sincere, faithful, consistent, and capable of regular and repeated renewal. Of course, just to know love's importance doesn't mean that one lives by love. There are many people who give lip service to the idea of love, people for whom loving is not a basic part of their lives. There are also plenty of hostile, ungiving, lonely, selfish people in the world, who have heard all about the value of love but cannot or will not allow themselves to love. And even though evidence suggests a strong relationship between being a loving person and living a long and happy life, some mean-spirited people endure to a ripe old age. There seems to be an exception to every rule.

For doctors, however, agape is one of their most important treatment resources. And while it obviously isn't necessary for therapists to believe in God in order to see something 'infinitely precious' in their neighbors, including their patients, it helps to do so, for such faith can only provide further comprehension and justification of and impetus to the process of healing.

PSYCHOTIC ILLNESSES

Not all the patients I've seen suffer with depression or wounded human relationships. I've seen my share of extremely disturbed, even psychotic patients, people out of touch with reality, hearing voices, frightened by appalling hallucinations, unable to think rationally, utterly bewildered, withdrawn, unspeaking, tortured by the unspeakable, lost in a sea of apathy and indifference. I have no doubt that, whatever psychological and interpersonal factors contribute to their illnesses—and they do, and they should never be overlooked—these patients are suffering with physical disorders that are just as physical as heart disease, cancer, tuberculosis, diabetes, or any other disease that we know and accept as being organic in its origins.

Their treatment often demands a kind of heroism of the part of the doctors and nurses who care for them. Courage to overcome fear. Determination. An unwillingness to give up. Enduring patience, and especially agape in the face of illnesses that sometimes seem positively inhuman.

I have never seen extraordinary miracles cure psychotic patients. But I have seen many cases of highly improbable cures. I recall one fifty-two-year-old woman—call her Caroline—both a friend and eventually a patient, who had suddenly and almost completely lost

her senses. In a few weeks Caroline had gone from a highly functioning woman to a person plagued with angry voices deriding her,
nearly irresistible urges to kill herself by jumping out of the four-
teenth-story window of her apartment, episodes of uncontrollable
tearfulness and occasional outbursts of rage, during which she
smashed a number of her valuable keepsakes. She was hospitalized
at once. After three months of futile efforts to relieve her symptoms
with a variety of medications, I was asked to confer with her doctors. Several other consultants were asked to review her case as well.
Without exception, they pronounced her incurable and recommended long-term hospitalization.

I dissented. I knew that Caroline's life had been exceptional. Generous and caring, she had devoted her life to helping others. She had
a deep faith in God. She had never before shown any signs of serious
mental illness. There had to be an answer. I recommended a course of
treatment that I seldom suggest, electric convulsive treatments.

I don't see many patients for whom shock treatments are necessary.
In the occasional situation where I think they would be helpful, I often find a great deal of resistance to accepting them from patients and
families alike, and from professional colleagues as well. The public
image of shock treatments is terrible, and it is, in my opinion, quite
unwarranted. Not only is it the most effective treatment for serious
depression when this condition has failed to respond to medication,
but it is one of the safest treatments in all of medicine. For older patients it is often a treatment of choice, since it lacks many of the side
effects and drug-drug interaction risks that accompany the use of antidepressants.

Reluctantly, Caroline's family agreed to go ahead. Her brother, an
investment banker, kept me on the phone for an hour, asking me over
and over again to explain how the shock treatments worked, wanting
to know why the other doctors hadn't suggested them, caustically
questioning my authority and experience. When he asked what the
worst side effects of the treatment were, other than recent memory
lapses that I had already explained, I told him that the worst that was

likely to happen was that she wouldn't improve. Heartened by this, he then asked why they had not been given to Caroline sooner.

Four weeks and eight treatments later, Caroline was well again, and she remained well for years thereafter, never again succumbing to any form of mental illness.

What's the miracle in this? The miracle is that she received the treatments at all, considering the initially loud opposition of her family and the committed pessimism of her other physicians. The miracle is that more than sixty years ago Ladislas Meduna, a Hungarian neurologist and neurpathologist observed that the postmortem brains of patients with dementia praecox (a form of schizophrenia) had fewer than the normal number of neuroglia, but that those of patients who had had epilepsy had markedly more. Neuroglia are the myriads of branched cells in the central nervous system that provide a supporting and communicating network for neurons which are the basis for thought, memory, emotion, and action. He theorized that artifcial seizures might help patients with schizophrenia. Meduna never established the validity of his theory, but, first using camphor, and later metrozol, to induce convulsions, he was able to produce a remission of illness in about half of a series of 110 schizophrenic patients whom he treated. In 1938, Italian psychiatrists Ugo Cerletti and Luigi Bini were the first to activate therapeutic seizures with electric current, a technique that was far less traumatic for the patients and which, in the ensuing years, has become quite sophisticated and very safe. While no longer used for schizophrenia, except for patients with "catatonic" withdrawal, stupor, and mutism, it is now considered a highly effective treatment for depressed patients whose clinical manifestations are quite complex, who fail to respond to antidepressant medications, and who are more advanced in years. It was no less a miracle that Ronald Kuhn, a Swiss psychiatrist, was open-minded and keen enough to note that imipramine, a tricyclic drug that had been developed and was being studied for its effect on the delusions and hallucinations of psychotic patients, actually relieved depression, and the era of antidepressant medication began.

I like to think of Caroline's dramatic recovery as one more example of divine providence, which, as philosophy professor Stephen T. Davis writes in *In Defense of Miracles*, is how God usually works. "An example might be God's guiding or strengthening or enlightening someone. This might happen through thoughts or feelings that God causes the person to have, perhaps through the words or actions of some other human being or through some natural event . . . . someone recovers from a serious disease, survives a dangerous accident, or happens to be in just the right place at just the right time for something important to happen."

9

Healing the Body

I n February, 1975, Teresa Patino was a nineteen-year-old woman living in Rionegro, Columbia, When she was five years old, she had stepped on a sharp object in a swamp. Lacking proper medical care, her leg became infected. She developed osteomyelitis. As a result, her right leg was warped and twisted from the knee down, and as she grew to adulthood, it was six inches shorter than her left leg.

As Dr. Francis MacNutt recounts, he, Bishop Alphonso Uribe; Father Carlos Aldunate, S.J.; Sister Jeanne Hill, O.P; Mrs. William Callaghan; and Alberto del Corral, a translator, prayed over Teresa for two hours. During that time, Teresa's crippled leg seemed to grow nearly an inch. The same night, they prayed again for two hours, and again, her leg seemed to have grown another inch and to slowly become less twisted. Two hours of prayer again the next morning, and the leg grew an inch more. The right foot, which was flat and had no arch to speak of, also grew and changed shape until the arch came in as in the normal foot. In a few hours, Teresa's toes had nearly doubled in size.

The team of healers began to appreciate that Teresa still felt hurt and rejected by the fact that her mother, who, being poor, had given Teresa over to others who could afford to provide medical care for her. They asked her to forgive her mother and prayed for healing of the girl's feelings of rejection. Later that day, they discovered that Teresa's brother had been seriously injured in an automobile accident some years before and that she had offered her crippled state to God if only he would spare her brother's life. Consequently, Teresa felt guilty about the healing that was taking place. The bishop used his authority as God's representative to free her from the effects of any such vow.

After the healing services were done, Teresa's leg continued to grow until there was only a half-inch difference between the two legs. Dr. MacNutt recounts: "—a doctor who examined Teresa said the bone was still broken and weak and counseled against walking yet." But Alberto, the translator, further recounts: "Shortly after her visit to the doctor, a group gathered again with Bishop Uribe for further prayer. As we laid hands on Teresa we noticed that the place where the bone was broken was quite warm and the lump greatly reduced in size. We prayed for about two hours and finally Bishop Uribe asked Teresa to stretch her leg and foot, an act which always caused a great deal of pain. Hesitantly, Teresa stretched out her leg and as she did so, the bone stayed in place for the first time in years. She felt no pain or discomfort as she moved her leg . . . Several days later she saw not one, but two doctors, both of whom confirmed that the bone had welded . . . Now, for the first time in 14 years, Teresa is walking again."

Dr. MacNutt tells of another healing in June of the same year. "—in June 1975, at the Oregon Camp Farthest Out (a kind of retreat) we began praying in a group for Bunni Determan, a lovely teenager who was encased in a neck brace because of a severe scoliosis (S shaped curvature of the spine)—after we had prayed for ten minutes—a change had taken place. So we kept praying for two hours, and by the end of that time most of the curvature at the top of the spine had been straightened out. The next two days, the group, including many of Bunni's teenage friends, prayed some more – another hour each day – and by the end of [the camp program] Bunni's back seemed about 80% improved. And with continued prayer by her mother and her friends she is now out of her neck brace and about 90% of the way to having a straight back."

These remarkable healings occurred nearly twenty-five years ago. Dr. MacNutt's book, *Healing*, was updated and reissued in 1999, but no new accounts of healings of this sort are described. One must conclude that amazing phenomena are really quite rare. Even at Lourdes, only sixty-two healings have been approved over 150 years, and noted writers on this subject offer very few first-hand examples.

Norman Vincent Peale, in his best-selling book of the 1950s, *The Power of Positive Thinking*, tells of a man with osteoma of the jaw, a bone tumor, who had been told it was practically incurable. A religious man, he began to read the bible more regularly. Over a number of weeks, the tumor grew less noticeable. One day while reading a passage, he described having a "curious inward feeling of warmth and great happiness." From that time on his improvement was more rapid, as the osteoma slowly but steadily disappeared.

Billy Graham has an example of healing through faith in his book *The Holy Spirit*. "God heals under certain circumstances in accordance with His will," he wrote. "My own sister-in-law is an outstanding example. She was dying of tuberculosis. The x-rays showed the seriousness of her condition, but she asked her surgeon father for permission to discontinue medical treatment because she believed God was going to heal her. It was granted, and some godly men and women anointed her with oil and prayed the prayer of faith. Then a new series of x-rays was taken, and to the astonishment of the physicians at the sanitarium she no longer showed any signs of active tuberculosis. Immediately she began to gain weight . . . Obviously she was healed . . . the healing came, not through someone who had the gift of healing, but through faith."

EVANGELISTIC HEALERS

Even the healing services held by such famed evangelists as Marie B. Woodworth-Etter (1844–1924), Aimee Semple McPherson (1890–1944) , Oral Roberts, and Kathryn Kuhlman (1907–1976), can claim credit for a few apparently substantiated cures.

George Orr had lost the sight of his right eye in 1926, as a result of an industrial accident. His vision had not actually been destroyed, but was seriously obstructed by a deep corneal scar. He was awarded workmen's compensation.

Twenty-one years later, on Sunday, May 4, 1947, while Kathryn Kuhlman was preaching, declaring that physical healing was just as possible as salvation, George Orr prayed: "God, please heal my eyes." To his astonishment, he felt a tingling in his right eye, "as though a mild electric shock were passing through it, " tears streamed down from it. When the service was over, he staggered outside, his inability to walk in a straight line possibly the result of what is referred to as 'being touched by the Holy Spirit.' Driving home, he noticed he could see the road markers. As they reached the top of a hill, the sunlight seemed to become brighter. Once home, he realized that he could see clearly out of his right eye. His optometrist confirmed that not only was the scar tissue gone, but also that the left eye had regained vision it had lost over the years as well.

But as with all faith healing preachers, Kathryn Kuhlman's work came under considerable criticism. Dr. William A. Nolen, a highly reputable and well-known physician, attended one of her meetings and was horrified to see a pretty, twenty-year-old woman "waving her leg brace and standing, with her pelvis tilted badly, on one good leg and one short, withered leg." She had been a victim of polio. "And now you're cured?" Kathryn is said to have asked. "You don't need it any more? You've taken it off?" To which the girl is said to have replied: "Yes. I believe in the Lord. I've prayed, and he's curing me."

Nolen obtained a list of the men and women who had claimed to have been healed at that meeting. He located eighty-two of them.

Twenty-three of them agreed to meet with him. He also followed up on cancer patients who had testified, but had not responded to his invitation. Nolen concluded that there had not been a single case of physical healing that day.

To counterbalance Nolen's published report, H. Richard Casdorph, M.D., an internist, carried out his own follow-up studies. One twelve-year-old girl named Lisa Larios had been diagnosed as having cancer of the hip socket. She had lost the ability to walk, and suffered with great pain. The doctors gave her six months to live. During Kathryn Kuhlman's healing service, Kathryn pointed in Lisa's direction and said someone in that area of the arena was receiving a cancer cure. Lisa, who did not know she had cancer, reported a warm sensation in her abdomen to her mother. "Stand and take your healing," Kathryn shouted, still not knowing she was addressing Lisa. Lisa stood up, started to walk free of pain, then ran to the platform. When she arrived home, she rode her bike. Two years later, x-rays and a brain scan showed no sign of her cancer.

One of Kathryn Kuhlman's most publicized healings was that of Captain John LeVrier, a Houston, Texas police captain and a Baptist deacon. He had been told in December of 1968 that he had a metastatic prostate cancer. At the healing service, Kathyrn Kuhlman pointed in LeVrier's direction, saying: "You have come a long way for your healing from cancer. God has healed you ... " The captain felt a wave of strength travel through his body. Overcome, he fell to the floor, a "slaying of the spirit." Presumably, this experience is a gift of the Holy Spirit. The person feels as light as a feather when he or she falls, and while they lie on the floor, they experience great peace and a sense of God's presence. This may occur whether healing accompanies it or not.

Sometime later, LeVrier was examined by an eminent radiologist at the M.D. Anderson Institute who could find no evidence of his previously diagnosed cancer.

The question is: are these healings so infrequent and inexplicable that they could entirely be explained on the basis of pure chance? According to Dr. Larry Dossey, author of several books on healing, the spontaneous remission rate for cancer is about one in 100,000. In the excitement of the moment, at these healing conventions, is it not possible that the disappearance of a malignancy might be triggered by a change in the body's natural defense system resulting in marked improvement or a total cure? What part, if any, does faith in God play as such in these unusual cures?

Dr. Larry Dossey, in his book *Healing Words*, relates a report of spontaneous remission of cancer by Yujiro Ikemi and his colleagues at the Kyushu University School of Medicine in Fukuoka, Japan in 1975. There were five patients in all. One, a seventy-seven-year-old man, suffering with adenocarcinoma of the stomach, refused surgery; he expressed the desire to serve God for his remaining years, and in a follow-up, five years later, his tumor had disappeared. Another patient, a thirty-one-year-old woman with metastatic cancer was quoted as saying, "I was not afraid of cancer. That was because I had my religious faith. But without it, I would have given in to the fear of cancer . . . . Because of this [disease], I was forced to an early mental awakening. I had been a stubborn person and I feel I had my corners rounded off by having cancer. Faith to me is not the attachment to life just wishing to be saved, but it is the gratitude to God, who saved my spirit. I [began] to live a real life since that time." The patient was reported to be in good health nine years later, with no evidence of cancer or metastases.

Dossey itemized four features that characterized these patients. Each had experienced a serious life crisis when they developed cancer. All had a remarkable absence of overt depression or anxiety, in four of the five cases because of intense religious faith. All gave themselves "totally" to the will of God and took measures to reconstruct their relationships with others, reducing long-standing self-centeredness and inflexibility.

By no means miracles in the extraordinary sense, these examples could add to the already substantial evidence that exists for the close connection between one's state of mind and physical health. Religious faith provides an important centeredness for the believer, and this sense of togetherness and meaning is a characteristic we physicians commonly see in patients who are successful in overcoming or making the best of any illness.

LAYING ON OF HANDS

The laying on of hands is an ancient healing ritual. In recent years, it is exemplified in a technique called Therapeutic Touch, which is a method theorized to balance and increase the body's energy to promote healing. It is not necessarily carried out in a religious context. Dr. Susan Wager, a physician, in her book *A Doctor's Guide to Therapeutic Touch*, attributes its development and introduction into medical practice to a nurse, Dr. Dolores Krieger, and Dora Kunz, past president of the Theosophical Society in America. Kunz is said to have been stimulated to explore its healing potential after having observed the practices of Oskar Estebany, a one-time colonel in the Hungarian cavalry. The colonel apparently discovered his ability to help sick people—on rare occasions quite remarkably, most of the time to a more modest, but nonetheless helpful degree—when he stayed up all night stroking and comforting an injured horse that was to be shot the next day, only to find the animal entirely well in the morning.

During therapeutic touch the healer's hands pass over the surface of the patient's body several inches to a foot away from it, even while the patient is fully dressed. The first step involves a search of regions where, in contrast to the warmth associated with a healthier emanation of energy, the practitioner feels coolness and stickiness indicative of an energy deficit. Then the task is to redirect energy throughout the entire body by the passing of hands, simultaneously visualizing the patient as well and sometimes imagining color, white or cobalt blue, streaming into the patient's body. The procedure takes about fifteen minutes; it is repeated over time, as often as required to accomplish the goals of the healing.

This technique presumably accelerates the body's normal healing processes. It seems to promote healing of wounds, fractures, and infections, improves breathing in patients with asthma, and enhances the immune system. Solid evidence of its effectiveness are sparse. The most obvious benefits are psychological—a reduction in anxiety and tension—with physical improvements that follow being consistent with the traditional concepts of psychosomatic interaction. In some reported cases, therapeutic touch sounds like a substitute for psychotherapy, with some patients suddenly gaining insights into themselves and their situations and initiating meaningful life changes as a result.

Dossey tells of one study of the laying on of hands in which the patients didn't even know that this was taking place. He describes an experiment carried out by Daniel P. Wirth. Wirth performed a double-blind study involving forty-four patients with artificially created full-skin-thickness surgical wounds. (Double-blind means that neither the subjects nor the experimenters know who is getting the real treatment and who is getting, in effect, a placebo, otherwise known as a "sugar pill.") This is standard operating procedure for assessing any form of treatment, and it is designed to reduce the influence of suggestion on the patient and bias on the part of the observer

The subjects in Wirth's study inserted their wounded arms through a circular cut-out aperture in the wall of the facility, beyond which they could not see. They kept them in place for five minutes. They were told that the purpose of this procedure was to measure "biopotentials" from the surgical site with a noncontact device.

A "noncontact" therapeutic touch practitioner was present in the adjoining room only during exposure for twenty-three subjects; the room was vacant during the sham procedure periods for the remaining twenty-one subjects. When she attempted to heal the wounds, she presumably held her own hands near the subjects, but did not touch them, remaining far enough away so that they would not detect any warmth or sensation frequently associated with such healing.

The results proved to be highly significant statistically. By the eighth day following exposure, the wound sizes of the "healed" subjects were significantly smaller than those of the untreated ones, and by the sixteenth day following exposure, thirteen of the twenty-three treated subjects were completely healed compared with none of the treated group.

Dossey does not say whether or not prayer or any form of invocation for God's intervention was part of the procedure. I assume not. He does suggest that certain individuals possess a still mysterious power to heal, whatever its origins may be. Most healers, like Kathryn Kuhlman, have been careful to proclaim that they did not heal themselves, but rather that God healed through them. Dr. Francis MacNutt believes that everyone has, to varying degrees, the potential for healing, a gift that is a divine gift, not a natural endowment, one that resides in God himself.

Essentials for Healing

Norman Vincent Peale, having investigated numerous cases of successful healing, concluded that five factors were invariably present.

1. A complete willingness to surrender oneself into the hands of God.
2. A complete letting go of all error such as sin in any form and a desire to be cleansed in the soul.
3. Belief and faith in the combined therapy of medical science in harmony with the healing power of God.
4. A sincere willingness to accept God's answer, whatever it may be, and no irritation or bitterness against his will.
5. A substantial, unquestioning faith that God can heal.

"In all these healings," Peale writes in *The Power of Positive Thinking*, "there seems to be an emphasis upon warmth and light and a feeling of assurance that power has passed through. In practically every case that I have examined, in one form or another, the patient talks about a moment when there was warmth, heat, beauty, peace, joy, and a sense of release. Sometimes it has been a sudden experience; other times a more gradual unfolding of the conviction that the healing has occurred."

Rev. Peale offered an example of one patient who had been operated on for cancer. "All precautionary treatments were taken," [the patient said,] "but the manifestations returned. As may be expected, I was terrified; I knew further hospital treatments were futile. There was no hope, so I turned to God for help . . . I had asked for this help one morning, as usual, and spent the day going about my household duties, which were many at that time. I was preparing the evening meal, all alone in the kitchen. I was aware of an unusually bright light in the room and felt a pressure against my whole left side, as though a person were standing very close beside me . . . . By morning, the improvement was so noticeable, and I was so free in my mind, that I was certain, and reported to my friend that the healing had taken place. That was fifteen years ago, and my health steadily improved until I am in excellent condition now."

Very few people appeared to have been healed of physical illness as a result of true miracles involving total exception to the natural law, recoveries that are instantaneous, complete, lasting, inexplicable. Most of us must rely on good medical care to get well, but all the evidence indicates that invoking the power of God in our efforts can make an enormous difference.

REVERENCE FOR LIFE

Albert Schweitzer was one of the twentieth century's most famous healers. He was born in 1875. As a young man he became a Lutheran minister, but his theological speculations—such as raising doubts about Christ's divinity, a central tenet of most Christian religions—placed him at odds with his church, and he chose to become a physician instead. In 1913, accompanied by his devoted wife, Helen Breslau, a nurse, he arrived in Africa as a medical missionary. He built a hospital at Lambarene in the French Congo and his work of healing consumed the rest of his life. Schweitzer was awarded the Nobel Peace Prize in 1953, at the age of 78.

In his prolific writings, Schweitzer makes no reference to miraculous healings, only to those achieved by the hard work of a dedicated surgeon. But if you're looking for miracles, you need look no further than his whole life's purpose to find one of the providential kind. I don't know whether he believed in angels, but he may well have encountered his angel in a small boat on the Ogowe river in 1915, as he described in his book, *Reverence for Life*.

At sunset of the third day, near the village of Igendja, we moved along an island set in the middle of the wide river. On a sandbank to our left, four hippopotamuses and their young plodded along in our same direction. Just then, in my great tiredness and discouragement, the phrase 'Reverence for Life', struck me like a flash. As far as I knew, it was a phrase I had never heard nor ever read. I realized at once that it carried within itself the solution to the problem that had been torturing me. Now I knew that a system of values which concerns itself only with our relationship to other people is incomplete and therefore lacking in power for good. Only by means of reverence for life can we establish a spiritual and humane relationship with both people and all living creatures within our reach. Only in this fashion can we avoid harming others, and, within the limits of our capacity, go to their aid whenever they need us.

10

Prayer

PRAYER IS THE BASIC METHOD of communication between man and God. Jews pray to God and Christians pray to God and His Son, Jesus Christ. Muslims pray to Allah, Hindus to Visnu (preservation and happiness) or Siva (the struggle against evil and the demons of destruction). Hindu philosophers believe there is one supreme principle personified as Lord (Isvara) or conceived as a neuter deity or an impersonal Absolute (Brahman); they conceive of a trinity consisting of Brahma, responsible for the creation of the universe, Visnu, and Siva. Buddhism is not a God-centered system of belief. It is more akin to a philosophy and spiritual practice designed to bring its believers to a state of perfection. Buddhists pray to the buddhas and Bodhisattvas, past and present, on their path of Enlightment.

American Indians would appear to be pantheistic, praying to many beings on earth, such as animals or birds, one of which might become an individual's guardian spirit, discovered through a dream or vision experience. But, in fact, they are not pantheistic. Most tribes believe in one God, the Great Spirit, whom they cannot know and hence cannot name or approach directly, so they do this through intermediaries. Black Elk, speaking with John G. Neihart, said: "We regard all created beings as sacred and important, for everything has a *wochangi*, which can be given to us, through which we may gain a little more understanding if we are attentive. We should understand well that all things are the works of the Great Spirit. We should know that He is within all things; the trees, the grasses, the rivers, the mountain and all the four-legged animals, and the winged peoples; and even more important, we should understand that He is also above all these things and peoples."

Most prayers follow a similar pattern—worship and adoration of God, repentance, asking for His forgiveness, thanksgiving, petition, and ultimate submission to His will. Muslim public prayer ritual, Salat, one of the five pillars of Islam, emphasizes worship of Allah and repentance for sin; private prayer, called du a, is the place for supplication and personal invocations. Hindus pray for the living and the dead, and ask their gods to help them in their material needs as well. Buddhist prayer primarily entails self-reflection and determined will, in an effort to achieve the five powers (bala) which lead to enlightenment and ultimately nirvana, the cessation of all interaction with manifest appearance. These are: faith to eradicate false views; effort to eradicate unwholesome views; concentration; absorption in the object of contemplation; and wisdom. When matters concerning health are involved, the object of one's meditation may be Bhaisajyaguru, the Healing Buddha, depicted as holding a lapis-lazuli (a healing stone) medicine bowl containing nectar in his lap, cupped in the meditation gesture of his left hand, to indicate the importance of medication for healing.

For the American Indian, symptoms of any illness whatsoever are seen as a disturbance in a normal balance and harmony to be restored through ceremonial 'chantways' of from two to nine or even fourteen days' duration. The chantway specific to the illness is determined by a special quasi-shaman diagnostician. Plumed prayer wands are used to compel the gods to come and be present with their curative spiritual powers. Religious practitioners of the Plains Indians are medicine men or medicine women. They employ curative herbs, but they have also received special sacred powers and helpers through vision or dream experiences, and are thereby qualified to guide others in the means to experience the sacred.

The Roman Catholic Church has renamed its sacrament for the sick and dying. It used be called Extreme Unction, and was reserved for those who were in immediate danger of death. Remember seeing, in war photos and films, the scene of the chaplain, bending over the fatally wounded soldier, anointing his forehead, and praying as he did so? In the past, if the priest arrived at your hospital room and suggested that you would do well to receive the sacrament, unless you knew you were at death's door, it could frighten you out of your wits. Now the sacrament is called the Anointing of the Sick, and, returning to early church practice, it is used for anyone who is seriously sick, physically or emotionally, but who still may have a real chance of recovery. In the Roman rite, the ritual consists of the anointing of the forehead and hands of the sick person. In the Eastern rite, other parts of the body are anointed as well, accompanied by the liturgical prayer of the celebrant (priest) asking for the special grace of this sacrament. Among the effects of this sacrament are:

- A uniting of the sick person to the passion of Christ
- The strengthening, peace, and courage to endure in a Christian manner the sufferings of illness or old age
- The forgiveness of sins, if the sick person has not been able to obtain this through the sacrament of Penance or Reconciliation
- The restoration of health, if it is conducive to the salvation of his soul
- Preparation for passing over to eternal life.

THE ROSARY

"Without thinking of what I was doing, I took my Rosary in my hands and went on my knees," said Bernadette Soubirous when her beautiful Lady first appeared to her.

At Fatima, Mary reportedly asked the three children, Lucia, Francisco, and Jacinta to pray the rosary and to urge others to do the same, to pray for peace and a return to the ways of God.

The Catholic rosary—which means a garland of roses—is made up of fifty beads (five sections of ten beads each), with a larger bead interspersed between each. The Lord's Prayer, followed by ten Hail Marys, is recited five times, silently or aloud, as one's fingers move from bead to bead. At the same time, specific Biblical events in the life of Christ and Mary are considered.

Five Joyful Mysteries are focused upon during Advent and up until Ash Wednesday and the beginning of Lent. The person praying meditates on:

- The importance of *humility*, as exemplified in Mary's acceptance of God's will, when the angel Gabriel informs her that she has been chosen to be the mother of Jesus.
- *Charity* to one's neighbor, in the Visitation, when Mary calls on her cousin Elizabeth who will soon give birth to John the Baptist.
- *God's love*, with the Nativity in Bethlehem.
- *The spirit of sacrifice*, exemplified by the Presentation of the Child Jesus in the Temple in accordance with God's law.
- *God's glory*, when, after He has been missing for three days, the twelve-year old Jesus is found among the teachers at the Temple, "doing His Father's work."

Five Sorrowful Mysteries are the focus of attention during the season of Lent. Here one meditates upon:

- *Repentance* for one's sins, by considering Jesus' Agony in the Garden.
- *A spirit of mortification*, by considering the suffering of Jesus as He is tied to a pillar and scourged.
- A desire for *moral courage*, while visualizing Christ being crowned with thorns.

• A desire for *the virtue of patience*, as one considers Jesus carrying his cross through the streets of Jerusalem.
• *The desire for Christ to be with you at the hour of your death*, as you contemplate His Crucifixion.

In the five Glorious Mysteries, said between Easter and the beginning of Advent, one meditates upon:

• Desire for strong *faith*, as one thinks upon the pivotal event of Christian belief, Christ's Resurrection.
• The virtue of *hope*, visualizing His Ascension to Heaven.
• *Zeal for the glory of God and His inspiration*, manifested in the Descent of the Holy Spirit upon Mary and the Apostles.
• *The grace of a holy death*, as one considers the Assumption of Mary into Heaven.
• *Special love and devotion to Mary*, contemplating her coronation as Queen of Heaven.

Recitation of *this* rosary is a Roman Catholic practice. But meditating upon the life of Christ, asking God's forgiveness for sin, and praying for such blessings as faith, hope, charity, courage, healing, and salvation are common to all who believe in Christ. So too is the practice of repetitive prayer. In recent years, Anglican prayer beads have become popular among a number of Protestants. These are made up of four groups of seven beads each, called Weeks, divided by four Crucifixion beads. The Weeks represent (1) creation, (2) the temporal week, (3) the seasons of the church year, and (4) the seven sacraments. In the Eastern Orthodox Christian Church woolen cords, with from thirty-three to 300 knots, are used primarily by the clergy to assist in prayer.

The origins of Bernadette's rosary are not clear. It has been traditionally attributed to the thirteenth-century friar, St. Dominic. However, well before his time it was common to use prayer beads to keep count of Kyrie eleisons (God have mercy), private or public recitation of the Psalms, and the Pater Noster (Our Father). The word "bead" is found in Chaucer and is derived from an Old Saxon word bede, which means prayer. It was only in the twelfth century that the angel Gabriel's salutation to Mary announcing the conception of Jesus became widely employed as a prayer, and it was only at the end of the fifteenth century that meditation on the joyous, sorrowful, and glorious mysteries of Christ's life were added.

Nor are Christians the only ones to use beads to keep track of repeated prayer or meditation. The Muslim subhah is made up of twenty-five, thirty-three, or 100 beads. Each one represents a different name of Allah. Each prayer is a tribute to His glory. A string of 108 beads is designed to help the Buddhist advance toward his or her ultimate enlightenment; each bead represents an earthly desire and prayer concentrates on the true self, purity, boundless eternity, and happiness of the Buddha.

SAINT JUDE

In my own life, at crucial turning points, especially when I have been ill, or when someone in my family or a friend needs help of any kind, I pray more often and more intently than usual, directly to God, or to Him through Jesus Christ. When things look especially grim, I also pray to the Father through an intercessor by the name of Jude. Many Christians exclusively direct their prayers to God or Jesus, and Catholics also pray to God through saints, whom they believe have God's ear.

Praying to St. Jude is considered especially effective when things seem hopeless. Jude was one of Jesus's twelve apostles. But in contrast to many of the others, not much is known about him. Writer and journalist Liz Trotta has written an excellent book about him called *Jude: A Pilgrimage to the Saint of Last Resort.* The name Jude in Hebrew was originally yehudhah, meaning "praised by the Lord." He was also called Thadaeus in the gospels of Matthew and Mark, from the Aramaic meaning chesty, heart, courageous, big-hearted. The traditional information about his ministry and martyrdom is not entirely reliable. In the third century, Eusebius, often referred to as the father of church history, related how, after an exchange of letters between Christ and King Abgar of Edessa, Jude journeyed to that kingdom, cured Agbar of leprosy, and converted him to Christianity. In the sixth century, a writer known as Psuedo-Abdias chronicled Jude's journeys to Persia, where St. Jude and St. Simon were eventually killed. In John's gospel, at the last Passover supper that Jesus and his apostles share, it is Jude who asks the question that continues to haunt so many of us to this very day: "Lord, how is it that thou wilt manifest Thyself to us, and not unto the world?" Christ's answer is curiously obscure: "If a man loves me, he will keep my words, and my Father will love him, and we will come unto him, and make our abode with him." What Jesus meant by this has been debated throughout the centuries. Trotta suggests that perhaps Jesus is saying "that the world is not to be persuaded collectively by signs and wonder, that fundamental changes happen in secret within individual human hearts . . . of revealing God's kingdom quietly by answering each lonely cry."

Trotta tells the story of Manuel Villafan. Villafan had struggled up from poverty in Spanish Harlem. In 1971 he set out to start his own company, manufacturing longer-lasting [cardiac] pacemakers. He was thirty-one, had no money, many debts, and a son in the hospital. Villafan happened to visit St. John's church in New Brighton, Minnesota, where he saw a Saint Jude prayer card in the pew in front of him. "It said two things," he recalls. "First, that Jude had been forgotten because of the similarity of his name to Judas Iscariot's, and, second, that one must promise to repay Jude by promoting his name."

He made the St. Jude novena there, nine days of prayer with daily mass and communion. Within weeks he found an investor. He encouraged as many people as he could to pray to St. Jude on behalf of his son, who needed a series of operations; his son recovered. His wife was pregnant at the time, and when a boy was born, he named him Jude. In 1976, he started a new business to make heart valves, and to honor St. Jude, he called it St. Jude Medical, Inc., and the company has been phenomenally successful over the years.

In the mid-1970s, I happened to be reading the listing of over-the-counter stocks in the *New York Times* and there was St. Jude. I blinked twice to be sure I was seeing it correctly. I located the company's headquarters in Minneapolis and telephone Manuel Villafan. I suppose the fact that I was a physician helped me reach him right away. He told me why he had named his company St. Jude, and I shared my own devotion to St. Jude with him. I then bought 400 shares of STJM and held it for more than twenty years. It's one of the best investments I ever made.

Most Americans are familiar with the story about the comedian Danny Thomas who seemed caught in a rut of playing cheap clubs and one-nights stands, whose prayers to God through the intercession of St. Jude seemed to have brought about his big break and launched him on his very successful career. In gratitude, Thomas helped to build the St. Jude Hospital for children in Memphis, Tennessee.

Throughout this country, there must be thousands upon thousands of people who believe that St. Jude helped them deal with problems to which there seem to be no obvious solutions. John Cardinal O'Connor, Archbishop of New York, is quoted by Liz Trotta as saying: "An awful lot of people feel lost and desperate, so it would not be surprising that they would at least be curious about this saint. Usually the opening question is, Have you heard of St. Jude? Is it true he can work miracles? I tell them, Of course. He is one of God's instruments."

Trotta also quotes Fr. Stephen Carmody, O.P., a priest from the Dominican order assigned to Sloan-Kettering Memorial Cancer Hospital in Manhattan, as explaining why many people may find it easier to turn to a St. Jude rather than approach God directly: "Theologically, [a particular young priest's] objections [to the need for an intermediary in praying to God] are no doubt very sound. But he hasn't been on parochial duty long enough to see how exhaustion, terror, diffidence, even sheer embarrassment may make an appeal to an intermediary less overwhelming than an appeal to a divine presence, or that prayer to an intermediary may indeed bring him closer to God than ever."

The church of St. Catherine of Sienna, to which Fr. Carmody is assigned, is across the street from the medical school I attended nearly fifty years ago. I discovered St. Jude there when I was twenty, and I've continued my devotion to God through his intercession ever since. I remain convinced that he has played a very significant role in my life, and, like Manuel Villafan, who acted to make St. Jude's name known by naming his heart valve company after him, I wear a St. Jude medal, which everyone can see when I'm in my bathing suit, and my automobile license plate reads STJD, short for St. Jude.

I have prayed, in one way or another, most of my life, usually directly to God, asking forgiveness for where I have failed; giving thanks for the many good things I have been given—talents, opportunities, family, friends, health, sanity; asking for a favor or two, for inspiration, for courage when the going got tough; for others whom I love, always, and sometimes even for people I don't particularly care about. It hasn't always been easy, but I prayed anyway. And even though I usually specified the things I was praying about, I also added that, in the end, God knew best, so His will be done.

Carl Jung, in *Psychology and Religion*, described leaving the answers to our prayers in God's hand. He considered this to be the essence of the religious experience when he wrote of his patients who had 'found' themselves: "They came to themselves, they could accept themselves, they were able to become reconciled to themselves and by this they were also reconciled to adverse circumstances and events. This is most like what was formerly expressed by saying: He has made his Peace with God, he has sacrificed his own will, he has submitted himself to the will of God."

11

∾

Scientific Appraisals of
the Healing Power
of Prayer

IN RECENT YEARS, a number of efforts have been made to
evaluate the effectiveness of prayer as an instrument of healing.
The vast majority of these suffer from methodological limitations and, in my opinion, none can be considered conclusive.

Dr. Larry Dossey has described many of these studies in his book,
Healing Words. Various experiments seem to point to a positive effect
of prayer on high blood pressure, wound healing, heart attack,
headaches, and anxiety. Prayer is also reported to influence the activity of enzymes, the growth rates of leukemic white blood cells, muta-
tion rates of bacteria, the germination and growth rates of various
seeds, the size of goiters and tumors in animals, rates of hemodialysis
of red blood cells, and hemoglobin levels, and the time required to
awaken from anesthesia.

Some of the results are intriguing; others are inexplicable. For example, in the Spindrift Studies, a more or less controlled study done in

Salem, Oregon, the researchers reported that "prayer" produced a reactivation of growth in mold on the surface of rice agar, after it had been stressed by rinsing in alcohol to damage it. Mold for which no such prayers were said, did not recover. Furthermore, direct prayer, in which the aim of restoring growth was specified was not as effective as open-ended prayer without any specific outcome in mind. (Does this imply that, with so many people praying on this planet, that the proliferation of molds will eventually reach astronomical proportions?) Here we also have an example of healing in which the faith of the patient, or in this case the mold, is not required for healing to occur, unless molds have a more complex psychic life than we have heretofore attributed to them. Perhaps all life forms have an instinct to survive.

In another experiment, two groups of mice were surgically wounded. A healer held the cages of half of them for fifteen minutes twice daily for two weeks, and this group healed significantly more than the controls. Enzyme system, fungi, yeasts, bacteria, plants, animals, and human beings—all seem to have been helped by healers who consider themselves conduits through which a healing flows from a higher power of some sort.

What is not clear throughout Dossey's presentation is what kind of prayer was actually involved in any of these illustrations. He has suggested that any type of prayer will do, whether the Lord's Prayer or meditation on a mantra. When he talks about an energy field of some kind that knows no boundaries of time or space, does he see the process of healing as Daniel J. Benor, M.D. defined it, as the "intentional influence of one or more people upon another living system without utilizing known physical means of intervention?" Mind over matter? Psychokinesis (moving physical objects by an act of will)? Telepathy (transferring thoughts and feelings to others across distances, without the use of a mobile phone)? Tapping some invisible cosmic force?

Personally I think there is merit to parapsychological investigations, into such phenomena as extrasensory perception or Kirlian photography, whereby energy waves seem to emanate from our bodies, varying in color and intensity as our health and emotional states alter. I believe we have only tapped our knowledge of very mysterious, yet quite natural, aspects of our existence. How is it that my own mother awoke in the middle of the night, frightened, sensing that something awful had happened, the very night that I was clinging to life, adrift in the Caribbean Sea? What explanation is there for the discovery of a treatise on clinical depression, printed in the year 1620 in Basel, Switzerland, by one Fredericus Flacht, years after I had chosen the study of depression as the main focus of my psychiatric research and had already published two books on the subject? As I was waiting to go in for surgery, what enabled my wife, while sitting in her bath, to envision that my prostate neoplasm had not metastasized and be convinced that I would be all right?

However, it seems to me that Dossey may have blurred the line between God-centered prayer and these rather remarkable human powers that we have only begun to appreciate. He sees our collective minds—or maybe it's one great big Mind—as not being completely localized to points in space, but rather, "unbounded and infinite in space and time—thus omnipresent, eternal, and ultimately unitary or one." Through this force, healing at a distance becomes possible. "All forms of distant healing, intercessory prayer . . . .diagnosis at a distance, telesomatic events, and probably non-contact therapeutic touch are included," he writes. It sounds like something out of Star Wars, the phrase "May the Force be with you" having just as much effect as prayers that clearly acknowledge God's power and presence, like "Our Father, Who art in heaven . . . ."

All this reminds me of something C.S. Lewis wrote concerning the nature of God:

When we point out that what the Christians [and of course Jews and Moslems] *mean* [by a Personal God], *some people say: "In that case, would it not be better to get rid of the mental pictures, and of the language which suggests them, altogether?" But this is impossible. The people who recommend it have not noticed that when they try to get rid of man-like, or as they are called, "anthropomorphic," images they merely succeed in substituting images of some other kind. "I don't believe in a personal God," says one, "but I do believe in a great spiritual force." What he has not noticed is that the word "force" has let in all sorts of images about winds and tides and electricity and gravitation. "I don't believe in a personal God," says another. "But I do believe we are all parts of the one great Being which moves and works through us all" not noticing that he has merely exchanged the image of a fatherly and royal-looking man for the image of some widely extended gas or fluid. A girl I knew was brought up by "higher thinking" parents to regard God as a perfect "substance"; in later life she realized that this had actually led her to think of Him as something like a vast tapioca pudding. (To make matters worse, she disliked tapioca). If God exists at all it is not unreasonable to suppose that we are less unlike Him than anything else we know. No doubt we are unspeakably different from Him; to that extent all man-like images are false. But those images of shapeless mists and irrational forces which, unacknowledged, haunt the mind when we think we are rising to the conception of impersonal and absolute Being, must be very much more so.*

THE EFFECT OF PRAYER ON RECOVERY IN PATIENTS IN CORONARY CARE

Cardiologist Randolph Byrd designed a study to evaluate the role of prayer to God in healing. In his ten-month experiment, Byrd assigned 393 patients admitted to the coronary care unit at San Francisco General Hospital to either a group (192 patients) for whom prayers were said by outside prayer groups, or to one (201 patients) who were not specifically remembered in prayer. Whether these were prayed for independently by friends and family is not known, but certainly no boycott on prayer was instituted. No one—not patients, nurses, or doctors—was informed about which patient belonged to which group. The prayer groups were given only the first names of their patients as well as a brief description of their illnesses. They prayed every day, but they were not told how to pray.

The outcome was remarkable and statistically very significant.

Those patients for whom prayers were said were five times less likely to require the use of antibiotics for complicating infections than the control group. They were three times less likely to develop pulmonary edema, a condition in which the lungs fill up with fluid as a result of the heart failing to pump the blood through it with adequate strength. None of them required endotracheal intubation—a procedure to facilitate breathing by means of a mechanical ventilator, whereas twelve of the controls did. Fewer died, although this did not achieve statistical significance. Even Dr. William Nolen, who had attended one of Kathryn Kuhlman's healing sessions and came away quite unconvinced, acknowledged that Byrd's study was quite impressive. "Maybe we doctors ought to be writing on our order sheets 'Pray three times a day," he commented. Every prescription requires a doctor to note the dosage of the medicine, the frequency with which it should be used, and how long it should be continued before stopping. This idea isn't too far away from the experiences of Dr. Francis Mac-Nutt, who reported that some patients seemed to require a higher dose of prayer than others in order to improve.

But are we arrogant trying to apply the rules of science to determine whether prayer works or not? Are we trying to put God to the test, rather than being guided simply by faith, which is what He always asks of us?

12

What to Expect of
Prayers for Healing

EVERYONE WHO WRITES ABOUT prayer and healing
insists that the most effective form of prayer involves a submission to God's will. "A more effective way to pray is to trust
in God's love for us and surrender the direction of our life to Him,"
wrote Joan Webster Anderson. Norman Vincent Peale described
prayer as " . . . man standing before God, his whole life open for God's
will to be done through him."

Not that it hurts to pray more directly for what we need too. I did-
n't know it at the time, but eight years ago, when I was going through
major surgery for prostate cancer, a woman named Hattie prayed for
me. Hattie, now in her eighties, took care of three of my children from
the time they were born. As they grew up and no longer needed the
same kind of looking after, she continued to come to our home, once a
week, doing some light house cleaning and laundry, having coffee and
conversation with my wife. Hattie was part of many family celebrations, Christmas holidays, birthdays, school graduations, for she was
very much family.

But Hattie didn't pray for me all by herself. Her Baptist church in upper Manhattan was part of a national network of prayer for the sick. Hattie put my name into the system and, even now, I am deeply moved by the thought of so many spiritual people asking God to be of help to me in my hour of need. And I am forever grateful that my recovery was what He had in mind.

Does this imply that God has a message center where all prayers are received, reviewed, and decided upon? Maybe. But some who do not think that God necessarily makes these decisions on an ad hoc basis have proposed that the answer to our prayers has been in God's mind forever, but that what that answer may be is contingent upon someone using his or her free will to pray.

The course of our lives may depend on how much of a role prayer has played in them, and here too, it is less an immediate response to an isolated request than one made by a Person with whom we have established a long term friendship.

In a sermon he preached at All Saints Episcopal Church in Pasadena, California several years ago, Rev. Clarke K. Oler, an old and very dear friend of mine, described prayer as "a gradual process of building a relationship with God, a progressive turning toward God over and over again in a thousand moments and ways until we reach the point where prayer isn't just something we *do* a couple of times a day, but a dimension of our whole life, of every thought and feeling." Clarke sees the goal of prayer not just to learn about God, but to see ourselves as the person He knows us to be, the person God loves . . . .

"None of us can compare our prayers with any one else. Each of us is unique, and each of our prayers are unique. Fifteen years ago I was lying in a hospital bed after an operation that the doctor said revealed an inoperable cancer. It was late at night. I stared at the ceiling filled with fear and a sense of utter helplessness. I had given up trying to pray for myself. God was a million miles away. In the darkness I heard God speak to me, not words, just an idea that formed itself in my mind with absolute clarity. How did I know it was God? I cannot tell you. The heart has its own mysteries; I just knew. God simply said that I would be all right. I knew instinctively that did not mean I would get well, but that it didn't matter. If I got well, I would be all right; if I died, I would be all right because I belonged to God. Everything that I was, and everything that I ever would be in the future was safe in God's hands. In that moment all my fear left me, and I closed my eyes and slept in peace."

WHEN PRAYER DOES NOT LEAD TO RECOVERY

While some people seem to be healed by prayer, others only slight improved, and many others not at all, are we justified, or are we presumptuous in concluding that if God does not cure everyone, no one is truly healed in His name?

If there is a God and we pray to Him for healing, do we enjoy an absolute right to be cured? I don't know why we would. After all, human beings have always been vulnerable to illness and the end of all life is death. At no time in the revelations of the Hebrew Scriptures or the New Testament is God described as having promised physical and mental health, wealth, and happiness in this world for everyone who believes and prays to Him. How and what He does is up to Him. All He does promise is that our prayers, if sincere, will be heard. If His will and our wishes coincide, all to the good. But if they do not, He probably has something else in mind, in the great scheme of things, or for each one of us in particular. As C. S. Lewis put it: "All prayers are heard, though not all prayers are granted . . . When the event you prayed for occurs your prayer has always contributed to it. When the opposite occurs your prayer has never been ignored; it has been considered and refused, for your ultimate good and the good of the whole universe."

Sir George Pickering in his book, *Creative Malady*, tells of several famous men and women, whose contributions to the human race might not have happened, were it not for some unremitting disease. "It became evident to me that an illness that is not debilitating or disabling, or threatening to life may provide the ideal circumstances for creative work. Its only rival is prison. Of that I have no first hand experience, but Bunyan made the most of it, as did Bertrand Russell." Sir George might well have added Miguel de Cervantes de Saavedra. He did not live long enough to witness the remarkable compassion and dedication to reconciliation that Nelson Mandela brought to the creation of a new South Africa; it strikes me as miraculous that Mandela was not surreptitiously killed, as happened to innumerable leaders throughout history, and lived to fulfill what would appear to be the will of God.

FLORENCE NIGHTINGALE

Florence Nightingale is one of several outstanding people Sir George selected to illustrate his thesis. She was born in 1820 in Devonshire, England, into a wealthy and well-connected family. When she was seventeen years old, as she later wrote in her personal diary, "God spoke to me and called me to His service." By the time she was twenty-four, she knew with certainty that her calling was to work among the sick. Her family angrily opposed her ambitions, but, undeterred she went forward in her career, which reached its early peak at the British army hospital at Scutari.

The Crimean War, in which England and France were pitted against Russia, began in March, 1854. In November of that year, Florence Nightingale, along with thirty-eight nurses (ten Roman Catholic nuns, fourteen Anglican sisters, and fourteen hospital nurses), arrived in the Bosphorus. The horrific unsanitary conditions of Barrack Hospital at Scutari were a rich breeding ground for disease, especially dysentery and cholera.

At first, the staff physicians were indifferent, even at times hostile to what they considered her intrusiveness, but as hordes of wounded and sick soldiers from Balaclava flooded the hospital, they asked for her help. They got more than they bargained for. With money at her disposal and important political connections, Nightingale wrought wonders. At her exhortations, the Secretary of War sent a Sanitary

Commission to Scutari, whose actions, as she later wrote, literally "saved the British Army."

Florence Nightingale's presence at Scutari seems providential, and her amazing heroism, fighting against the ravages of contagious disease and the recalcitrant military bureaucracies seems miraculous indeed.

But it is the next phase of her life that exemplifies how her own illness set the stage for her radical transformation of the profession of nursing. After she returned to England, to worldwide acclaim, she grew weak and emaciated, and was confined to her rooms. She was convinced she had only a few months to live. She was then only thirty-seven years old. She did not die, but for the next twenty-four years she remained an invalid, necessarily avoiding social distractions, including all but limited contact with her family whom she experienced as her nemesis. Her incapacity gave her nothing but time to write and write, and pursue her determined efforts to reform the British system of health care. She actively directed the Royal Sanitary Commission on the Health of the Army in India, and, in the process of insisting on accurate reporting of illnesses among the soldiers in India and analyzing the information with the aid of Dr. Farr, a statistician, gave birth to the present science of epidemiology. At home, she successfully pressed for legislation that would create separate institutions for the sick, the insane, the incurable, and children.

And, of course, she continued to work for the establishment of nursing as a profession of dignity and respect.

Following her mother's death in 1880, Nightingale seemed to become less intense, more mellow. Her health slowly improved as well; on nice days, she could occasionally leave her rooms for a stroll with a friend. Now sixty-four years old, her eyes began to fail, and by the time she was seventy-one, she was completely blind. In the end, her mind began to fail, and she died in August 1910 at the age of ninety.

Sir George Pickering makes the point that Florence Nightingale's "disease" restricted her in such a way that it eliminated any and all distractions that might interfere with her life's mission. He implies that had she enjoyed good health all along, she might well have failed to accomplish all that she did. Probably so. He offers a psychiatric diagnosis to explain her condition, psychoneurosis.

But Sir George was not a trained psychiatrist and, of course, he never had the chance to evaluate Florence Nightingale for himself. I would not be surprised if she suffered from post-traumatic stress disorder, a relatively recent psychiatric diagnosis, considering the awful conditions under which she labored at Scutari and the unremitting confrontation with death, disease, and the horrors of war. It's also quite possible that she had contracted a primarily physical disorder, beyond the recognition and skills of the physicians of her time.

What matters here is that the failure to recover in so spiritually rich a person as Florence Nightingale enabled her to accomplish far more than she might have been able to do if well. " . . . it contributed to her legend," wrote Sir George. "The Lady of the Lamp was a more romantic figure in the form of an invalid recluse, whose influence was known to be immense, than it would have been had that person been constantly in evidence."

Louis Braille

Louis Braille is another example of a serious disability setting the stage for a major contribution to mankind. He was born in Coupvray, France, near Paris, in 1806. As a boy of four, he pierced one of his eyes with an awl, a sharp pointed tool, in his father's shoe workshop. His eye was destroyed, and some time later, he lost the ability to see out of his other eye as well. He was totally blind.

At ten, he went to a school for blind boys in Paris. In 1821, when Louis was twelve, a soldier named Charles Barbier visited the school. He demonstrated a system he had invented called "night-writing," which consisted of twelve raised dots that could be combined to represent different sounds and could be used by soldiers passing information to one another at night without speaking and thus giving their positions away. The idea captured Louis' imagination, and he developed the idea into a system that would allow the blind to read. The first book in Braille was published in 1827, when he was eighteen.

Louis taught at the school where he had been a student until his death from tuberculosis in 1852, at age forty-three.

However, the Braille system might not have won worldwide recognition were it not for the efforts of Thomas Rhodes Armitage, a Sussex-born surgeon who served in the British army in Crimea, and probably knew Florence Nightingale. Dr. Armitage had experienced a temporary impairment in his vision when he was a medical student in London. In 1860, at age thirty-six, he again suffered seriously diminished vision, forcing him to resign from active medical practice. This must have represented a grave disappointment for him, but being a man of deep religious faith and of independent means, Armitage chose to devote his career to helping the blind. "I cannot conceive," he wrote, "any occupation so congenial to a blind man of education and leisure as the attempt to advance the education and improve the condition of his fellow sufferers."

Together with three blind men, one of whom had been an artist before losing his sight, he formed a society that would eventually be known as the Royal National Institute for the Blind, and which today is one of the largest Braille printing houses in the world. His prayers too were undoubtedly heard and answered, not by affording him a cure, but by inspiring him to make such a wonderful contribution to the ability of blind people to learn and live more fully.

DEATH A FORM OF HEALING

Death can be a form of healing. "When patients whose bodies are tired and sore are at peace with themselves and their loved ones, they can choose death as their next treatment," wrote Dr. Bernie Siegel in *Love, Medicine, and Miracles*. "Often at that time they have a 'little miracle' and go on living for a while, because there is so much peace that some healing does occur. But when they die, they're choosing to leave their bodies because they can't use them for loving anymore."

Joan Webster Anderson tells of a mother who prayed for the recovery of her eleven-year-old son with cancer. God did not seem to answer. As he was dying, her son said, "I'll make a rainbow for you, mom." After a week in a coma, he died in the night, his mother by his side. As the morning sun rose over a hill, its light hit a little ornament that hung on his hospital window, creating a rainbow. She sensed that this was somehow an answer to her prayer, and, inspired, she began writing love letters with cards and toys to sick children.

I've asked a number of my religious friends about their experiences with prayer and healing. One of them related this: "My sister was a beautiful, black-eyed little girl of nine when she died . . . her death from pneumonia devastated my family. My parents were faithful at church and had prayed urgently for her recovery, but that was not to be.

"A few days after her burial, my mother was going through my sister's things on her bedside table. There was the little New Testament that sister received from her Sunday School class, and which she loved to read, especially in those final few weeks. My mother picked it up. It fell open to the place where my sister had placed the ribbon and marked a passage. She read: If you love me, you will not grieve, because I go to my Father who is in heaven. Those words from St. John settled upon mother's aching heart as a benediction. The message was clear. All was well with my sister; she had known that it would be so before she died, and wanted our mother and father to know it too."

PART V

Miracles of Discovery

One of God's Many Messengers

*Born in Alliston, Ontario, on November 14, 1891, he was raised
in a home that encouraged inquisitiveness, resourcefulness, persis-
tence, honesty, and godliness. He went to the University of Toronto
intending to study divinity. But he chose the study of medicine instead. During the first World War, he served as a medical officer
and was awarded the Canadian military cross for bravery, for
heroically attending wounded soldiers while wounded himself. He
was trained to be a pediatric orthopedic surgeon, but his practice
was far from thriving, so, in 1920, he took a position in the department of physiology at the University of Western Ontario. On
October 31, at two in the morning, Frederick Banting was suddenly inspired with the idea that was to lead to his being awarded
the Nobel Prize in 1923, a knighthood in 1934, and the survival
of millions of men, women, and children who otherwise might have
died tragic deaths from the disease known as diabetes.*

*By the early nineteen hundreds, scientists had already made the
connection between the islets of Langerhans in the pancreas and diabetes, but they had not been successful in isolating the active ingredient necessary for the control of sugar metabolism. The digestive
juices of the pancreas destroyed the hormone before it could be ex-
tracted. But what if it was possible to stop the pancreas from working and still keep the islets of Langerhans functioning? What if
surgically ligating the pancreatic duct would destroy the cells that
produced trypsin while still allowing what would later be called
insulin to survive?*

*Like the man in Jesus' parable in the gospel of St. Luke, who
tenaciously knocked on his friend's door until he was finally given*

the food he sought, Banting badgered the skeptical head of the department of physiology at the University of Toronto, J.J.R. MacLeod, until, in May 1921, he was given the laboratory space and equipment he needed for his experiments. Working together with Charles Best, a medical student, and later J. B. Collip, a biochemist, he succeeded in his efforts. The first patient to benefit from insulin was a fourteen-year-old boy who would otherwise have died of diabetes, and within a year, researchers had developed a safe and potent extract of insulin in commercial quantity

Those who knew Sir Frederick Banting have described him as a kindly, generous, spiritual man, with a strong sense of fairness. He came very close to refusing to accept the Nobel Prize because his colleague, Charles Best, had not been selected to share it with him. During the Second World War, he served as a liaison officer between the British and Canadian medical services and died in a plane crash in Newfoundland at the age of fifty.

13

Medical Revelations

IN THE HEBREW SCRIPTURES and the New Testament, God miraculously reveals Himself to human beings. In Revelations, He wants us to know more about Him and what He expects of us.

Divine Revelation, as such, ended with the death of the last of Jesus' Apostles. But I think that God may offer us a different kind of revelation too, one with small 'r' if you will. All discoveries—fire, bronze, Galileo's observation of the earth circling the sun rather than the sun circling the earth, the technology for space exploration— are, in my opinion, miraculous in their own right. They ultimately serve to help us master life here on earth, relieve our sufferings, and create a context within which we can grow spiritually in this world and in preparation for the life to come, even though their connection to our spiritual lives may not be immediately apparent. And, even as in the healing process where it does not seem necessary for the patients themselves to possess a strong sense of faith, so too faith does not seem to be a requirement for scientists who make important discoveries.

There's an old adage: "God will provide." What will God provide?

New knowledge of our material universe? New insights into ourselves? Antibiotics to combat our historical enemies, streptococcal infection, tuberculosis, plague, leprosy? Machinery permitting us to fly through the air and span continents in a matter of hours? Technology whereby we can communicate with each other instantaneously anywhere in the world? All of the above, and more. But He alone knows when we will come to enjoy the benefits of such revelations, and to what extent *they are answers to the prayers of millions upon millions of people from the beginning of time.*

Louis Pasteur

The 1936 film, *The Life of Louis Pasteur* starring Paul Muni, left a lasting impression in my mind, particularly the scene when, in 1879, Pasteur, returning to his laboratory in Paris after spending the summer in Arbois, discovers that the culture of chicken cholera bacteria that had been left standing all that time had lost his virulence; when inoculated into healthy animals, the germs failed to produce the expected results. He then injected the same chickens with a fresh dose of cultured material, and again they did not become ill. Pasteur immediately recognized the importance of this observation, one that was reminiscent of Jenner's use of cowpox vaccination to prevent or ameliorate the dreaded smallpox infection. Not only did Pasteur's work set the stage for understanding the nature of immunity, but it also provided a method for the manufacture of vaccines.

I saw the movie with my parents. My father, recognizing my enthusiasm for it, had a number of three by five notepads of paper printed up for me; at the bottom of each page was a quotation from Pasteur: "Chance helps those who are prepared." From a closer look at Pasteur's life, one might also say that prayer also helps those who are prepared.

In Patrice Debre's excellent book, *Louis Pasteur*, translated into English by Elborg Foster, one gains a great deal of insight into the mind and character of this remarkable man, a laboratory scientist and a healer on a grand scale. Pasteur's discoveries changed the lives of all humanity. He literally revolutionized medicine. He demonstrated the microbial origins of illness, developed various vaccines including one for rabies, and insisted on sanitary conditions for patients to reduce the risk of infections, such as those that accounted for the high rate of deaths among women delivering children. He created a model for rigorous research and its integration with what doctors practice in their office and hospitals.

But Pasteur's personal life is equally intriguing.

In 1868, at the age of 46, he was suddenly stricken with a condition that left him exhausted, unable to speak or to move the limbs on the left side of his body. Over the next few months, he gradually improved, but he was never to regain complete use of his body. One may suppose that Pasteur had suffered a stroke, affecting the right part of his brain, but one that left his intellectual faculties intact. This event occurred eleven years before his discovery of the immunity conveyed by attenuated chicken cholera bacteria. Had his mind been affected by his illness, or had he died of it, none of his other wonderful achievements would have happened. Others might have picked up where he left off, but where and when? Was it God's will that Pasteur's contributions to humanity's difficult progress should be primarily his own?

Did Pasteur pray for his recovery? We do not know. We can be sure, however, that his devout wife Marie did.

In the second half of the nineteenth century positivism was in fashion, a philosophy related to the system of Auguste Compte, who wanted to establish a new social system based on a "religion of humanity," in which everything became a science. Pasteur set himself in direct opposition to ideas of Compte as well as the advocates of scientism, such as Claude Bernard and Emile Littre, partly because of his dedication to the experimental method in research, partly because of such ridiculous notions as Compte's disapproval of the microscope as an instrument of investigation, but most important because of positivism's inherent denial of the existence of God.

Pasteur wrote, " . . . the positivist conception of the world does not deal with the most important positive notion of all, that of the infinite. Beyond that starry vault, what is there? More starry skies, granted. But beyond that? The human mind, impelled by an invisible force, will never cease asking: 'What is there beyond?' . . . Whenever anyone proclaims the existence of the infinite—and no one can escape it—he fills that assertion with more of the supernatural than there is in all the miracles of all religions; for the notion of the infinite has the double characteristic of being inevitable as well as incomprehensible . . . The idea of God is a form of the idea of the infinite. Where are the true sources of human dignity, of liberty and modern democracy, if not in the notion of the infinite before which all men are equal?"

Did Pasteur pray for his work? We do not know. However, many of his close colleagues—Jean-Baptiste Bouillaud, Octave Terrillon, Charles Monod, Edouard Quenu, Just Lucas-Championniere—were devout Christians. Surely they did their share of praying for his success.

Louis Pasteur died on September 28, 1895, at the age of 72. He spent his last days at Villeneuve-l'Etang, the remains of a small chateau in the village of Marnes-la-Coquette, parts of which the French government had assigned to him for his experiments on the prevention of contagious diseases. Members of his family read to him accounts of Napoleon's last battles—Pasteur's father had been a devoted follower of Napoleon, a sergean-major, awarded a *chevalier de la Legion d'honneur* for bravery at Bar-sur-Aube in 1814. They also read him scenes from the life of Saint Vincent de Paul.

His final wish was a testimony of his love. "May my children never stray from their duty and continue to give their mother the tenderness she deserves."

A Brief History of Medical Revelation

Louis Pasteur is but one in a long line of figures throughout history who have miraculously served to help heal our wounded hearts and bodies. Many of the principles of healing can be traced back to earliest history, and, from the beginning, these were intermingled, for better or worse, with religion.

The Sumerian/Asyrian healing tradition was largely omen-based, and used divination based on inspecting the livers of sacrificed animals for diagnosis, since the liver was regarded as the seat of life. There were three types of healers, a seer specializing in divination, a priest who performed incantations and exorcisms, and a physician who employed drugs and carried out surgical procedures. Disease was seen as being caused by spirit invasion, sorcery, malice, or violating taboos, and always gods were involved, meting out punishment in the form of sickness..

In ancient Greece as well, religious healing was prominent. The great plague of Athens (430–427 BC) was seen as due to the wrath of the gods and relief was sought through prayer. It was then that the famed physician Hippocrates (c.450–370 BC) voiced his contempt for those who attributed illness to divine intervention in the affairs of humans and called for physicians to take a more naturalistic approach to understanding its causes and cures. He saw health as an equilibrium, and illness as a disturbance in that equilibrium, resulting from an undue concentration of fluid in a particular part of the body—blood, yellow bile, black bile, and phlegm. These were called the humors, and the mainstay of his treatments consisted of diet, blood-letting, and changes in life-style. Galen, born of Greek heritage in 129 AD, was known as the great physician of Rome. Following in the tradition of Hippocrates, he emphasized the importance of the doctor-patient relationship and the critical role of trust in the healing process.

By the tenth century, medicine flourished in Egypt and the spread of Christianity introduced a spiritual dimension to helping the sick, whose care was seen as a central duty of the religious life. Monasteries became medical centers, where medicine was practiced according to what was then known of the art. Brother Cadfael, Ellis Peters' fictional monk, who returns from the Crusades to join the Benedictine order at the Abbey of St. Peter and St. Paul at Shrewsbury, is portrayed as mixing his medicinal herbs and offering wisdom and solace to those in need, when he wasn't busy solving crimes. Cadfael's real-life counterpart was an eleventh century nun, Hildegard of Bingen, who, as Abbess of Rupeertsberg, practiced medicine, using the curative powers of herbs, stones, and animals.

Healing shrines proliferated, such as Bury St. Edmunds in England and Rocquemadour in France. Relics of saints were believed to possess healing powers, and the saints themselves were proclaimed as guardians of various parts of the human body and to be invoked as intermediaries for various disorders. For example, St. Luke was a physician; Damian and Cosmas became the patron saints of medicine; St. Anthony would be called on to help patients with erysipelas; St. Sebastian for pestilence; St. Vitus for chorea; St. Pergamin for cancer; St. Margaret of Antioch for women in labor; St. Blaise for protection against diseases of the throat.

Many of these beliefs continue to this day. For many years now, I've spent several winter weeks on the pleasant Caribbean island of Anguilla. The feast of St. Blaise on February 3 usually occurs while I'm there, and I routinely make a point of having my throat blessed at St. Gerard's church in the Valley. (Of course, were I to develop a severe cough that wouldn't go away in a few days, I would also immediately consult my physician.)

In the thirteenth century, we get a glimpse of the beginnings of medicine as we know it today. Roger Frugardi of Parma produced his *Practica chirurgiae*, a study of anatomy and surgery, and the glass workers of Venice introduced spectacles, a truly remarkable event at the time. Gutenberg's invention of the printing press in the fifteenth century facilitated the dissemination of medical knowledge.

The compound microscope, without which Pasteur could not have made his wonderful discoveries, was invented in the sixteenth century, and Paracelsus substituted an alchemical model for the humoral model of Galen, becoming one of the precursors of chemical pharmacology. Paracelsus also proposed the notion of a "vital force [that] is not enclosed in man, but radiates around him like a luminous sphere, and [which] may be made to act at a distance. In these semimaterial

rays, the imagination of man may produce healthy or morbid effects."
Sound familiar?

The seventeenth century was a time of greater progress. Thomas
Syndenham, an English physician, suggested that atmospheric conditions could affect the nature of illness; it was he who named scarlet
fever and differentiated it from measles. William Harvey published
his ground-breaking anatomical description of the motion of the
heart and blood in animals; Cinchona (Jesuit's bark), the active ingredient of which is quinine, used in the treatment of malaria, was
brought from Peru to Europe; and George Ernst Stahl put forth his
life force or vital principle concept wherein the body is guided by an
immortal soul.

In the eighteenth century, Mary Wortley Montagu introduced
smallpox inoculation in England. James Lind found the cure for
scurvy in the English Navy (fresh citrus fruits); Franz Anton Mesmer
introduced hypnotism; William Withering introduced digitalis,
found in the foxglove plant; Phillippe Pinel in France and William
Tuke in England began the era of treating mental illness with kind-
ness and care instead of incarceration, chains, and displays before
laughing crowds on Saturday afternoons at Bedlam; and, as the century came to a close, Edward Jenner developed smallpox vaccine using material from cowpox.

In the nineteenth century—Pasteur's century—Rene-Theophile-
Hyacinthe Laennec introduced "mediate auscultation" by means of
the stethoscope, and J.J. Lister invented the achromatic microscope.
Another scientific breakthrough occurred in 1839, with the introduction of photography. In 1844, Horace Wells, a dentist, used nitrous
oxide as an anesthetic; two years later, in 1846. William Morton used
the anesthetic ether for the first time. In 1847, Ignaz Phillip Semmel-
weis called for physicians to wash their hands well before delivering
babies to reduce the risk of infection, only to be ridiculed and punished by his medical colleagues. (Pasteur was soon to take up the
cause.) The opthalmoscope was invented in 1850 by Hermann von
Helmholtzd. In 1865, antisepsis was finally introduced in surgery by

Joseph (Lord) Lister. Robert Koch identified the bacillus responsible for tuberculosis. Wilhelm Konrad Roentgen discovered x-rays in 1895, and the following year, 1896, the Italian physician Scipione Rive-Rocci introduced the sphygmomanometer, known to us as the cuff and gauge our doctors use to determine the level of our blood pressure. In the final years of the century, Ronald Ross discovered that malaria was transmitted by mosquitoes of the genus Anopheles and a remarkable new drug was introduced, called Aspirin.

It is in our own twentieth century, building on the work of the nineteenth, that medical advances seem to explode. William Einthoven introduced electrocardiography in 1901. Between 1906 and 1912, the work of Frederick Gowland Hopkins and Christiaan Eijkman led to the discovery of vitamins. Frederick Banting and Charles Best discovered insulin in 1922. In 1926, George Minot and William Murphy found that pernicious anemia could be cured by eating large amounts of raw liver, which led to treatment first by liver extract, and, in 1949, by the active agent, vitamin B12.

In 1928, Sir Alexander Fleming noticed that a mold of the genus Penicillium stopped the growth of bacteria in one of his colonies that had been contaminated by it; it will be another twelve years before penicillin is successfully tried in humans, and it will be mass produced during the Second World War largely as a result of the insistence of President Franklin Roosevelt. In 1944, Selman Waksman discovered streptomycin, the first antibiotic effective against tuberculosis. Antibiotics were even found to cure the eternally dreaded leprosy. Jonas Salk developed a vaccine against polio.

Since 1950, there has been an avalanche of new antibiotics, and drugs of every sort—for high blood pressure, heart disease, diabetes, allergies, pain management, depression, anxiety, schizophrenia, and more. Sir John Chanley made hip replacement a routine operation; the heart-lung machine required for cardiac surgery was developed, cardiac bypass surgery for coronary artery disease was made possible in the 1960s, as was the first successful heart transplant by Dr. Christiaan Barnard in South Africa. By the 1980s we had endoscopic, keyhole surgery, and with the discovery of DNA (deoxyribonucleic acid), a rapid increase in genetic research with the promise of genetically-based treatments for a variety of diseases in the not too distant future.

Medicine as we know it is very much a product of the last two-hundred years, growing in knowledge, effectiveness, and promise at a nearly geometric rate during the past half century. In one way, it would seem to be a logical progression, from microbes and antisepsis to antibiotics; from anatomy, physiology, and anesthesia to advanced forms of surgery. In another, it can be seen as miraculous, the average life-span more than doubled, the quality of life enormously improved, as if, after thousands of years of suffering, human beings have been given special blessings, not unlike manna in the desert during the flight of the Israelites from Egypt.

However, I'm not sure we really appreciate how much we have received or where these wonders have come from. Consistent with the materialism of our age, we take credit for having made these amazing advances all on our own, and fail to see them as God's providence and continuing revelation about the nature of our world, to say nothing of his mercy and compassion.

14

*Revelations about
Disorders of the Mind*

GREAT STRIDES HAVE BEEN MADE over the past hundred years in our understanding of the nature of mental and emotional illness. But the existence of such disorders has been acknowledged from earliest times. The origins of wild, melancholic, bizarre behaviors were thought by some to be due to divine intervention, by others to possession by evil spirits, and by others, such as Hippocrates, to a mixture of psychological and biological causes not unlike medical thinking today. For example, he noted that grief might trigger insanity, but he thought that melancholy madness resulted from an excess of black bile. Galen believed that mania was a disease of yellow bile; he envisioned it as a "hot" disease and recommended cooling the body as a form of treatment. Soranus attributed mania to a number of factors, many of which we now recognize as symptoms of the disorder rather than its causes, feeding on each other as the patient is propelled into a more and more serious state of confusion and disorganization—serious, persistent insomnia; excesses of anger, sadness, fear, or superstitiousness; severe tension accompanying intensely ambitious pursuits; sudden shocks; or reversals of fortune. In those days, the caretakers' main job was to prevent patients from injuring themselves or others. There were no psychiatrists. There were no asylums. It was largely up to the families to look after their own.

With the emergence of the Christian era, certain monasteries and religious houses cared for the mentally deranged, where a more humane approach to such patients was taken, consistent with the teachings of the church regarding the care of the sick. Of course, exorcism was occasionally employed, but more routinely gentleness was the treatment of choice. Paul of Aegina, in the seventh century, anticipated a modern-day approach to calming disturbed patients by recommending the use of music therapy. Mildly distressed individuals had their confessors and spiritual counselors to whom they could turn, the medieval equivalent of the contemporary psychotherapist. But for the seriously deranged, there was little hope for cure, unless, as we now know does occur, the acute episode cleared up on its own (or perhaps in answer to prayer).

No doubt, a number of mentally ill persons were burned as witches prior to the eighteenth century, when a more enlightened world gave us the asylum. Bethlem Hospital, known commonly as Bedlam, in London was one of a number of such abominations, gothic horrors complete with cruelty, neglect, whips, and chains. Thomas Monro, the chief physician at Bethlem, was himself a severe alcoholic and generally insane.

Amid such a hideous scene, a kinder and more noble approach to psychiatric patients reemerged in the early nineteenth century. In France, Philippe Pinel, a devout Roman Catholic, was given responsibility for the insane at the Bicetre in 1793. Pinel considered that the insane behaved like animals because that was how they were regarded. He removed the chains that bound most of them, and his efforts were, by and large, a great success. He introduced what was called *moral treatment*, an approach to care that considered the emotional and intellectual aspects of his patients. He emphasized gentleness and a strategy of *hope*, wherein patients need not be thought of as doomed to a life of animality, that there might often be an element of the human that could be preserved and enriched. Moral treatment, anticipating what today is called cognitive therapy, proposed to end the faulty thinking supposedly involved in insanity by distracting patients from their delusions, by involving them in useful labor, or ameliorating disordered emotions by direct, authoritative confrontation by the doctors.

In England, the York Retreat was established in 1796. Here a quiet, comfortable, supportive environment was created. A model of family life was employed. Patients and staff lived, worked, and dined together. Recovery was promoted by various rewards and punishments, by offering praise when warranted and blame as well, all done in a most humane manner. By such means, the caretakers sought to *diminish helplessness and restore the patient's morale and self-control.*

Throughout the 1800s the pendulum of effort to discover the nature of mental illness swung heavily toward physical causalities. In mid-century Germany, Professor Wilhelm Griesinger insisted that "every mental disease is rooted in brain disease," and saw this conceptualization as both encouraging opportunities for solid research and also restoring dignity to patients who had so long been stigmatized for their illnesses. He anticipated the National Institute of Mental Health and the National Association for the Mentally Ill, an organization of patients' families, the primary goal of which is to promote research into the biochemical and physiological causes of mental disorders and the development of new treatments based on discoveries in these areas.

Emil Kraepelin felt that heredity played an important role in mental illness, and it was he who developed a classification of mental disorders that distinguished between schizophrenia (dementia praecox) and manic-depressive psychoses—a classification that has proved to be so vitally important in diagnosis and treatment today.

FREUD AND JUNG

In 1896, Sigmund Freud gave a lecture in Vienna in which he proposed that his hysterical female patients had been subjected to prepubescent sexual seduction by their fathers, and that repressed memories of such assaults were what caused their problems. The following year he changed his mind, deciding that his patients' seduction stories were figments of their imaginations. What was really going on, Freud concluded, was a little boy's sexual love for his mother and jealousy and hate toward his father, or, in the case of little girls, their desire for their fathers and hostility toward their mothers. These were called the Oedipus complex and the Electra complex respectively. And the world of psychiatry and psychiatric patients, of high school teachers and university professors, of novelists and playwrights and movie makers was never the same since. Only now, nearly a hundred years later, are we professionally and culturally beginning to remove ourselves from the powerful grip of his deterministic theories.

Freud did make some real contributions to our understanding of the human mind, to be sure. His concept of the repression of early traumatic memories into the unconscious where they remain alive and capable of influencing our adult thoughts and emotions, and his use of free association and dream interpretation to access these so as to relieve the sufferer from their destructive power made us realize that we are not always masters of our fate and captains of our souls. Something else, within us, may compromise our ability to use our free will as effectively as we might. "Where id was," Freud noted, "there ego shall be." In other words, resolving these old wounds could set the stage for a greater degree of freedom in choosing the direction of our lives.

At the same time, his theory promulgated a general feeling of pessimism, determinism, and helplessness, since few of us would ever have the time, energy, motivation, or money to lie on analysts' couches for years on end engaging in a form of damage control. Such negativism was further compounded by Freud's outspoken denial of the existence of God, whom he saw as nothing more than the human being's projection of the wish for permanent parental care onto a basically indifferent universe made up of mere matter.

Initially, Carl Jung was one of Freud's disciples, but he was unable to accept many of his teacher's key ideas, such as the sexual origin of the neuroses. And so he developed a psychology of his own, which included personality typology, a theory of a collective unconscious in which each of us possesses latent memories that go back to our ancestral past, imprints having to do with the survival of the species, archetypes of mothering, fathering, hunting, defending, building, being a member of a community, even religious archetypes. In 1912, the French sociologist, Emile Durkheim came upon some of the same notions about religion as Jung, when he suggested that religion and its images were representative of a genuine truth emotionally (as opposed to intellectually) experienced. For Jung, the symbolic language in dreams, myth, folk tales, and religions contained a kind of psychological truth, born of psychic substance, and carried into an image-world that comes back to us, repeated again and again in different cultures, regardless of their separation in space and time, many of which have no historical affiliation with each other.

Jung felt that professionals who counsel or carry out therapy should attend to the spiritual issues of those who come to them for guidance and care. Finally, now, mental health professionals seem to be getting the message. Jung is credited with contributing to one of the key elements in the twelve steps of Alcoholics Anonymous and similar programs: turning oneself and the attainment of one's sobriety over to a higher power beyond oneself. For example, the third step calls upon people to "make a decision to turn their will and lives over to the care of God as they understand Him; the eleventh "seeks through prayer and meditation to improve one's conscious contact with God." Overcoming an addiction to alcohol or drugs is hard to accomplish, and doing so can readily be considered a miracle in the ordinary sense. In a letter of appreciation, AA's cofounder, Bill Wilson, wrote to him, citing a conversation that Jung had had with a Roland H. in which he told Roland H, who had a seriously drinking problem, that his hopeless state was beyond medical or psychiatric help. Jung is said to have qualified his statement, advising the patient that "there might be [hope] provided he could become the subject of a spiritual or religious experience—in short, a genuine conversion . . . that he place himself in a religious atmosphere and hope for the best."

I personally don't know enough about Jung to know what he really believed. Maybe he genuinely believed in God, but concealed his faith. Then again, he may have been agnostic. Perhaps he had a "tapioca" vision of God, like the one described by C.S. Lewis. Perhaps he saw Him as one more myth, an archetypal necessity for the preservation and advancement of mankind. Curiously enough, Jung claimed to have contact with spirits. He called these archetypes. He claimed that he was inspired in what he wrote by such entities, especially his own familiar spirit whom he named Philemon. "Philemon represented a force which was not myself," Jung wrote. "In my fantasies I held conversations with him, and he said things which I had not consciously thought. For I observed clearly that it was he who spoke, not I . . . Psychologically, Philemon represented superior insight, He was a mysterious figure . . . At times he seemed to me quite real, as if he were a living personality."

Maybe Jung was just eccentric. Or, maybe he was in touch with an angel and simply failed to recognize or acknowledge him for who he was, though he probably knew that Philemon was the name of an early Christian, to whom the imprisoned St. Paul wrote his final epistle.

THE PSYCHOBIOLOGICAL REVOLUTION

Contemporary psychiatry has moved away from Freud and Jung (in spite of Jung's current public popularity) to engage in a relentless hunt for new medications to treat the emotionally disturbed. And it has been a remarkably successful pursuit, from the benzodiazpines to relieve anxiety to both traditional and atypical antipsychotics to treat psychoses; from the heterocyclic antidepressants and the selective serotonin reuptake inhibitors to relieve depression to lithium and the anticonvulsants to alleviate mania and stabilize mood swings in manic-depressive (bipolar) disorder. Even as the first part of this century was devoted to unearthing the psychological issues with which emotionally distressed individuals were wrestling, the second half has aimed squarely at the workings of the brain and nervous system, biogenic amine transmitters delivering messages from one cell to another, such as norepinephrine, dopamine, and serotonin. We even have tomography technology to photograph the cerebral hemispheres and the lower centers of the brain in Technicolor so as to picture differences in color—and hence activity—between the brains of psychiatric patients, people in various intense emotional states, and the rest of us, calmy listening to music or watching movies on television. I sometimes wonder what our brains would look like while we were listening to loud, jarring music or viewing the violence that's so much a part of the nightly news.

What's losing ground, however, is the understanding, empathy, humanity, and practical psychological exploration that used to be an integral part of our care of patients. These are steadily being replaced by a more stringent medical model of diagnosis and treatment that is erroneously thought to be more cost effective. And the spiritual lives of patients continue to be given little attention.

All that's wrong about the system, however, is matched by a lot that's right. When attending to patients' psychological and interpersonal issues, prescribing appropriate medications, and working to help them recognize and develop their inner strengths, including their spiritual potential, are done in an integrated fashion and carried out by a well-trained, experienced, empathic, and humble physician or therapist, I can honestly say that treatment options for the mentally ill have never been better.

If you can persuade physicians to make use of them. If you can reduce the stigma that surrounds them. If you can get politicians, lawyers, managed care administrators, and the media to stand back and adopt a more intelligent, helpful, and compassionate approach to mental illness. And if you can get mental health professionals to be well prepared to fulfill their responsibilities, more willing to admit to what they do not know and still must learn, and more receptive to the patient's interpretation of what he or she is going through. This can be accomplished only by a solid appreciation of the part that religion and spirituality play in the lives of us all.

15

Revelations
in Our Own Lives

PSYCHOTHERAPY IS A PROCESS that involves a gradual unfolding of knowledge about ourselves and our worlds. It is a journey, of limited duration, during which one looks inwardly to discover thoughts, feelings, emotions, behavior patterns, perceptions, philosophies, choices—all of which have helped shape the people we now are now. This is done aloud and in the presence of another person, a so-called therapist, who is there to listen, understand, direct, and offer new ways of looking at the past and new strategies to deal with the here and now and the future as well.

With few exceptions, people who begin psychotherapy do so because they are in pain. You might seek psychotherapy because something has gone terribly wrong, suddenly—like the death of someone you love, a serious career reversal, betrayal by a trusted friend, divorce, a heart attack, an automobile accident in which you were driving and your girlfriend in the front passenger seat was killed—and you have been unable to come to terms with how it is affecting you. Or perhaps nothing seems to have worked out for you for years—crippled by fears, lacking self-confidence, experiencing moods of desolation, loneliness, unrealized dreams, dissatisfaction in spite of material success— and you finally accept the misery of your life and reach out for help.

Invariably you ask the question: Why? Why is this happening to me? Am I a weak person? Am I losing my mind? Is it bad luck? Or bad genes? Why have I been singled out for disaster, for suffering, for a nervous breakdown?

The last thing that might occur to you is that your circumstances may be God's providence in your life; that your pain and willingness to seek help represents a unique opportunity for healing that you may not have been able to accomplish on your own; a chance to learn how to deal with life in a much more effective manner than you ever have before. I'm convinced that, for many patients, starting therapy is exactly that. To understand and appreciate this goes a long way toward reducing the embarrassment and shame that most patients carry with them to the consulting room, and offers an important "positive spin" to the experience they are about to have.

More than this, it offers the essential element of hope. While no intelligent and honest physician can ever promise to cure anyone beyond a doubt, instilling hope for some level of improvement is part of every doctor's job.

INTRINSIC RELIGIOUSNESS AND RECOVERY FROM DEPRESSION

Dr. Harold G. Koenig carried out a study of the effect of "intrinsic religiousness" on the outcome of clinical depression in a series of patients over sixty years of age. These patients were not only depressed, but they also were suffering with a variety of physical illnesses as well. Of a large number of variables that he considered, only five characteristics independently predicted the speed with which the depression remitted. The most significant of these was intrinsic religiousness, namely the extent to which people with a strong sense of inner faith find their master motive in their relationship with God. This may be expressed as "My faith involves all of my life," or "In my life I experience the presence of the Divine," "My religious beliefs are what really lie behind my whole approach to life," or "One should seek God's guidance when making every important decision." It has nothing to do with participation in religious rituals. It has everything to do with how important one considers his or her relationship with God to be.

Speculating on how a strong religious faith might have helped these patients recover from depression and deal more effectively with their physical disorders, Koenig suggests that religious beliefs provided them with a world-view in which suffering had a meaning and purpose, and also that their beliefs provided an indirect form of control over circumstances. For example, he notes, they reported that through prayer they could influence God who was all-powerful and could either change their health situation for the better or facilitate their adaptation to the condition.

I am reminded of one deeply religious patient, a forty-year-old man named Stephen, whom I saw some years ago and found it necessary to hospitalize because of the severity of his depression. He told me of standing in the shower, the water pouring over him, literally aching with melancholy in every cell of his body, wanting only to die, when the image of Christ on the cross entered his mind. "My suffering is nothing compared to yours," he thought. "I offer mine up to you. Please help me. Please." For a few moments, he felt tremendous relief, and, although his depressive pain soon returned, it never reached the intensity it had had previously. Within a few weeks, with rest, recreation, psychotherapy, and antidepressants, he felt renewed.

Not only did Stephen find strength and coherence in his faith at this critical juncture in his life, but he realized fully that this was an opportunity for him to examine his past and present life and find new and better ways to cope. His eyes, which had previously been closed, were open to learn forgiveness toward a wife who had left him for another man, although not before he had the chance to admit to and resolve the deep hurt and anger he felt about this betrayal.

He began to ask how he himself might have contributed to his plight. With the help of his therapist, Stephen came to realize that he had been so involved in pursuing his career as an investment fund manager that he had neglected to give his wife the outward signs of affection and consideration that any marital relationship requires. He saw that the origins of his behavior lay in the model of family life that his own parents had provided—an overindulgent mother who doted on his every whim and expected nothing in return, and a father who was remote and unapproachable, whose love was primarily expressed by giving material things, but with the expectation of gratitude in return. One gift that both his parents did nurture in him was his faith. Stephen had been brought up to believe in God, and Jesus, although sometimes he wondered why his parents' behavior did not seem to be more in keeping with what they professed, especially when it came to their apparent lack of affection for each other.

A LITTLE KNOWLEDGE OF OURSELVES AS WE WERE IS NOT ENOUGH

Each of our lives is filled with opportunities for revelation and growth. Because of our very human limitations, we can never know all there is to know about ourselves or anyone else for that matter. As Sir Henry Harcourt Reilly, T. S. Eliot's psychiatrist in his play *The Cocktail Party* observed: "Most of us live on a little knowledge of ourselves as we were."

But a little knowledge of ourselves as we were is not enough to find our way through the maze of life. As we evolve through the life cycle, from childhood to old age, we are bound to hit bumps in the road, some slight enough to give us a mere bounce, others profound enough to throw us into an abyss of anxiety and confusion. Some of these are inherent stages in the process itself, like growing up, getting married, having children, reaching middle age, and beyond. Others are thrust upon us, like hordes of Assyrians plunging down on the plains of Judea—untimely deaths of people close to us, being fired from jobs we thought to be secure, being survivors of earthquakes or tornadoes, being cast aside by a husband who'd rather be with a younger woman, imprudently putting our savings in risky investments only to see them sink to a tenth of their original value, and, of course, being told by the doctor that we have a serious illness with an unclear prognosis at best.

These events are part of the vulnerability of being human. We can interpret them as pointless tragedies or we can look upon them as opportunities to become more than we were before. We can look at them as chance events, bad luck, rotten destiny, not getting the breaks, a cruel, unjust twist of nature or even the heavy-handed the wrath of some uncaring God delighting in our miseries. Or we can look upon them as catalyst in the never ending journey of personal growth.

"I'm this close from declaring bankruptcy," Ryan said, squeezing the thumb and forefinger of his right hand together. "I've been looking for work for nearly eight months. Nothing. It's not easy in your fifties. I still have one kid in college. My wife works, but she doesn't make enough to support us."

I could see the anger in his eyes. 'Why did you come to see me in the first place?" I asked. It was his third visit. I'd spent the first two sessions finding out as much as I could about him, and I felt intuitively that I shouldn't have asked him that particular question earlier.

"I don't know. Because my wife insisted on it. I've been depressed, but I don't see what you or anyone like you can do about it. You're not a placement agency."

"I might be able to help you some other way," I suggested.

"Like how?" he asked defiantly.

"Like getting you to own up to what you're really feeling and do something about it."

He sat there silently for a couple of minutes. Then he began to cry, not little tears trickling down his cheek, but real sobbing.

When Ryan had pulled himself together again, he stared straight at me. "So now you know how I feel," he said.

"Actually I do. And I know that how you feel is keeping you from finding solutions. In fact, I wonder if how you feel is what got you into this trouble in the first place."

He looked surprised.

"Being depressed, I mean," I went on. "From what I already know about you I suspect you were having problems long before you lost your job that may have contributed to what happened."

Ryan covered his mouth with his hand and took a deep breath. "I haven't been myself in a long time," he said, "not since Jerry—that's my oldest son, he's twenty-four—got involved with drugs."

"When was that?"

"Seven years ago. He was seventeen."

"How is he now?"

"I don't know. I don't even know where he is. The last time we heard from him he was arrested in New Orleans for picking a fight at a bar. He was drunk."

"When was that?"

"Over two years ago. Peggy and I assume he's alive or we would have heard something."

"How many other children do you have?"

"Two. A daughter, twenty-two, and another boy, eighteen. They're doing fine. But . . . ."

"Like the one sheep who's missing," I said.

"Don't quote that stuff to me," he said, raising his voice. "Peggy's always going to church and praying, and I keep telling her there's no one up there listening."

"Sorry. I was just using a common analogy. I mean, even though everything else is all right in your life—or at least, it was until you got fired—it stills hurts. Your son that is."

Ryan sat silently for a couple of minutes. Then he asked, "So, where do we go from here?"

"We find out more about you and everyone else in your world. We find out how and why you've lost your spirit—it must have taken a lot of brains and hard work to get an engineering degree and reach the position you had with your company. And maybe we'll have to look at this as a biological problem as well. I mean, maybe you'd be best off taking a medication, an antidepressant."

"That's going to get me a job and bring my son back in one piece?"

"I think it will definitely help you find the energy to locate another job. As far as your son is concerned, I have no idea . . ."

When I had taken Ryan's initial history, he had told me that he was Catholic. Obviously, he had little use for his religion at this point in his life. As he saw things, God, if there was a God, had clearly let him down.

"When I asked you, you told me you were a Catholic," I said. "Did that mean anything to you at some other time in your life?"

"When I was a kid. I was an altar boy. But then, around eleven, I was late for Mass one morning when I was supposed to serve. The priest was furious. He hit me with his open hand hard over my left ear. He hurt me badly. I couldn't hear out of that ear for a week. My parents wouldn't do anything about it. I thought, what kind of a religion is it that talks about loving your neighbor and doing good and then has priests who go around hitting little kids. I thought, I don't need that."

"I can understand how you felt."

"Peggy tells me I should forget about it. I should pray. But no way!"

"Have you ever thought of forgiving the priest? I mean, looking at him for what he was, maybe twisted, maybe someone who just lost control one day when an altar boy was late and did something he regretted much of his life? Separating your ideas about God from the shortcomings of some of those who think that, because they wear black suits and white collars, they're special and don't have to account for their behavior the way you and I do?"

"No," Ryan replied honestly.

"Why not do that? If you were a confirmed atheist, I would never have pursued this line of conversation with you. But I don't think you are. Certainly your wife isn't. Let go of it. Put it behind you. Try to think of God as a powerful ally, even a friend."

"I can't promise anything," he said

"That's okay. But if you could, you might feel some of your strength returning and more hope and be better able to deal with things. But even if you can't, I can help you. I'd like to see you once a week, to talk, and I'd like you to start taking sertraline, one a day. It's an antidepressant. In a few weeks I think you will really begin to feel a lot better, if not before."

He nodded. "Okay. But not because I believe you can do anything. I'll do it for Peggy's sake."

"I don't care why you do it, as long as you do it."

Four weeks later, as I had predicted, Ryan was feeling considerably better. He was again pursuing job leads, and in another three months he had landed a position as good as the one he had lost. No miracle here. The efficacy of psychotherapy and the antidepressants have been well established.

It's in the realm of his relation to God and his discovery of the importance of the gift of forgiveness that one might say an ordinary miracle had taken place.

"That's not the only grudge I used to carry around," Ryan admitted to me. "I used to be really thin-skinned. I had a lot of resentment toward a lot of people over the years. When you told me I should consider forgiving that priest whose name I don't even remember, I thought it was impossible. But I did. And then I found I could forgive the others too. And I feel a new kind of happiness . . . free . . . hopeful . . . for the first time in years. I even think that Jerry will shape up and come home some day, but I know that that's out of my hands." He smiled at me. "So I pray about it," he said.

Ryan learned the lesson of forgiveness and was restored in his faith as a result of suffering an increase in depression following the loss of his job. A thirty-four-year-old woman who had been very much wrapped up in herself learned the importance of healthy humility and the value of giving as well as taking in relationships after her boyfriend of three years told her he simply couldn't commit himself to her, although he claimed not to know why. A twenty-nine year old man who is miserable because the lady he thinks he is in love with seems unable to give him a straight answer whenever he proposes marriage comes to realize that the relationship has been more or less a one-way street; it's his second such involvement and he suddenly sees that he has a penchant for attaching himself to women who are very conflicted about men. He even traces his vulnerability to growing up with a mother who was alternately loving and rejecting, given to unpredictable rages, and who used devious ways in an effort to control her children long into their adulthood.

Carl Jung once pointed out that many of the middle-aged people who came to see him were in crises because, over the years, they had cultivated only part of their personalities while neglecting the rest. They were not "whole." One may have become highly intellectual and analytic in his approach to life, but the inherent intuitive and emotional aspects of his being were sadly atrophied. Another may have lived with powerful intuition and a strong concern for other people, but sorely lacking common sense. The predicaments in which they found themselves and which led them to consult him represented a unique opportunity to develop the other sides of themselves and move closer to being more complete as human beings. And he felt that a drying up of one's spiritual self was at the heart of the despair in which so many felt so lost. Restoring it was the physician's legitimate goal, for, after all, the notions of "wholeness" and "holiness," and even that of "healing," come from very similar ancient roots in our language and our thinking.

PART VI

Faith
and
Resilience

Over the great city,
Where the wind rustles through the parks and
    gardens,
In the air, the high clouds brooding,
In the lines of street perspective, the lamps, the traffic,
The pavements and the innumerable feet upon them,
I Am: make no mistake — do not be deluded.

Think not because I do not appear at the first glance —
    because the centuries have gone by and there is
    no assured tidings of me that therefore I am not
    there.
Think not because all goes its own way that therefore
    I do not go my own way through all.
The fixed bent of hurrying faces in the street—each
    turned towards its own light, seeing no other —
    yet I am the Light towards which they all look.
The toil of so many hands to such multifarious ends,
    yet my hand knows the touch and twining of them
    all.

All come to me at last.
There is no love like mine;
For all other love takes one and not another;
And other love is pain, but this is joy eternal.

Over the Great City EDWARD CARPENTER

16

The Power of Faith

When Elisha sends a messenger to Naaman to
tell him that if he wishes to be cured of his leprosy he
should wash in the Jordan seven times, Naaman is at first
incredulous and, in fact, angry, but he does as he is bid and "his flesh
was restored like the flesh of a young boy, and he was clean." When
Jesus heals the two blind men, he says: "According to your faith, let it
be done to you." When the woman who had been bleeding for a
dozen years was cured after touching his garments, Jesus says to her:
"Daughter, your faith has made you well; go in peace, and be healed of
your disease." When Norman Vincent Peale recounts his observations
on healing, he cites as one crucial element, "belief and faith in the
combined therapy of medical science in harmony with the healing
power of God."

Dr. Bernie Siegel speaks of four faiths essential to recovery from or
successful living with illness: faith in oneself, faith in one's doctor,
faith in the treatment, and spiritual faith.

Dr. Francis MacNutt gives greater latitude to the power of faith:
" . . . faith in God's power to heal may rest in the person praying for
healing, the sick or troubled person asking for help, or even when no

one in particular seems to have faith." Alexis Carrel, describing miraculous healing at Lourdes notes: "There is no need for the patient himself to pray, or even to have any religious faith. It is sufficient that someone around him be in a state of prayer."

Faith has many dimensions. You can believe in many different things, from democracy to love to worldly success to the dominion of God. The faith a husband and wife put in each other, their trust, their loyalty is an example of faith on a very human level. When St. Paul says, "It is by faith that we are saved" he is speaking of faith on a spiritual level, and quite clearly referring to faith in Christ.

James W. Fowler in *Stages of Faith* approaches this subject from a broad viewpoint. He describes faith as a "dynamic process arising out of our experiences of interaction with the diverse persons, institutions, events and relationships that make up the 'stuff' of our lives . . . It unifies our lives' force fields." Fowler traces the evolution of faith through sequential life stages, from infancy to adulthood, pointing out how our orientations to life are profoundly influenced by our images of power—parents, governments, God—and the particular powers with which we align ourselves to help us master life's many difficulties in what is really a very dangerous world. Our faith is shaped by our centers of values, the contents of what we believe to be important for a sense of self-worth, such as accumulating wealth, serving others, taking part in a political revolution, or surrendering to the will of God.

There is a close relationship between the ability to believe in God and his healing power and the ability to believe in anything at all. Psychiatrist Smiley Blanton put it this way: " . . . it is difficult for a person who did not have an adequate relationship with his own parents in childhood to have a supreme faith in God, for the worship of God has always been a projection of the parent-child relationship." It's important not to confuse Blanton's comments with the antitheistic thinking of Sigmund Freud, who insisted that God was nothing more than an illusion and that a healthy person was one who had resolved his or her neurotic dependency on such a super-figure, and could face reality for what it was, whatever that may be.

Throughout my own psychoanalysis with Dr. Bertram Lewin, I believed in the process and I believed in him. Together, we examined many aspects of my life. I talked about my relationships with my childhood heroes, my parents; on balance, these were pretty good, although I didn't realize how good until I was a great deal older and wiser. And even though we seldom discussed my religious faith—which he did not share, but for which I always sensed him to have sincere respect—I feel that the psychological benefits I gained from this experience contributed to the spiritual resilience I enjoy today.

THE ABILITY TO TRUST

What Smiley Blanton was talking about is the intimate relationship that exists between a person's ability to believe—to trust, to have confidence in, to be loyal to—another person and his or her earliest experiences of childhood. Parents who respect and love each other, who know how to reconcile differences, forgive hurts and let go of resentments, and work to understand each other, and who genuinely love their children and offer them the models and guidance they require to grow into healthy adults, set the stage for a sturdy faith. On the other hand, an unloving, angry, pessimistic home environment has the opposite effect, even as suffocating a child with too much control, even in the guise of love, readily sets one up for being afraid of domination by anyone, including God.

There are many other circumstances that can affect a youngster's ability to trust, and hence, to believe, as they gradually come into contact with people beyond the family members who influence them. Teachers, for example, can represent reliable, caring adults, winning children's confidence and helping them become more confident in themselves, inspiring, conveying the wonder and excitement of learning. Or they may be insensitive, punitive, or models of indifference, indulgence, or injustice. The young child, watching carefully, gradually coming in touch with his or her own feelings, naively trusting, searching to distinguish what is real from what is not, cannot help but be buoyed up or profoundly disillusioned by what he or she encounters here.

With adolescence, peer pressure and societal pressures begin their determined infiltration into the young boy or girl's sense of what is right or wrong, what can be counted on and what cannot, what to believe in or whether to believe in anything at all. I have seen children's trust utterly demolished by their parents' divorce. I have seen youngsters who have engaged in sexual experiences when they were far too young and ill-prepared react with a deep sense of rejection, disappointment, guilt, resentments, and betrayal, leaving them diminished, confused, unsure as to where or how to really trust again.

During childhood and adolescence the content of faith also begins to take shape. If your family is very materialistic, values worldly success and riches above anything else, you may adopt the same goals or rebel against them, depending on your temperament and the nature of your relationship with them. It's not likely that you will be completely unaffected by their attitudes and behavior. If they value service to others above all, you may follow in their footsteps or make a 180-degree turnaround; putting your own needs above everyone else's may become your credo. If you're exposed to a healthy devotion to God, with family and others holding their relationships with Him to be at the center of their beings, through which all that happens in their lives, for better or worse, is perceived and understood, then chances are that this will also be the content of your faith. If you are submerged under a mountain of rules and rituals that stifle your creative energies or continually faced with a concept of God as an angry power more concerned with punishing wrongdoing than with loving and forgiving, it's easy to see how your faith may become infected with fear or why you might seriously question the idea of a god altogether.

FAITH IN PSYCHOTHERAPY

Faith then is very much a human quality that comes into play in all our interactions with others and colors our expectations of ourselves and of what lies ahead in our lives. People who come to see me as a psychiatrist are not coming in search of miracles. They aren't looking for God's intervention, as such, in their contact with me. What they are hoping—if they aren't too depressed to hope—is that I am a caring, competent physician who can effectively help them find their way out of whatever morass they're in, relieve their suffering, reconstruct their lives, and restore some meaning to them.

What often amazes me is how some patients consult me without knowing very much about me, professionally or personally. Sometimes they're referred by former patients or physicians who are familiar with the quality of my work. Occasionally they've read one or another of my books, which do reveal something about how I think and practice. But every now and then, patients arrive who have found my name on a list of psychiatrists, and choose me because my office happens to be convenient to their office or home. What do you want to know about me, I'll ask them. More often than not they have few, if any, questions. So I proceed to tell them a little about my medical background and how I approach treatment. I never cease to be surprised by the level of gullibility that certain people manifest, an indiscriminate trust that could easily lead to disaster. It's something to work on, an incredibly immature faith that is ready to offer itself to almost anyone who seems willing to pay attention.

Trust is a *sine qua non* of any successful interaction between doctor and patient. The more you know about the person to whom you intend to extend your trust, the more confidently you can do so.

FAITH IN GOD

Pascal once said that "If there is a God, he is infinitely incomprehensible, and we cannot know what he is." That's true, if we are left to our own devices. But God has given us some evidence of his existence, in the creation of all things to begin with. And in other ways as well, miracles being one.

Belief in God requires faith. In 1870 The Vatican Council defined faith as a "supernatural virtue by which, guided and aided by divine grace, we hold as true what God has revealed, not because we have perceived its intrinsic truth by our reason, but because of the authority of God who can neither deceive nor be deceived."

In *What Is Faith*, Eugene Joly writes: "If we are to believe the revelations of God and men who speak to them, such as the apostles, God must guarantee them to us in some way . . . a double signing on God's part, one of an external kind, visible to the unbeliever and verifiable, apparently, by him . . . The first of these signings is miracle . . ."

"But the foundation of our faith cannot rest upon miracles alone," Joly goes on. Something more is needed. A spark. A commitment. A sense of comfort and security.

And what such faith provides is a center around which to organize our lives. "Let the world do its worst," advises Norman Vincent Peale, "we know God is with us and we are not dismayed. The sense of God's presence steadies us, it gives us an anchor in the storm, and provides a reservoir of personal power. I do not mean that we will get this steadiness merely from some theological idea about God or some vague belief in Deity; but if we love God as a friend."

As a friend? Since I began to take angels more seriously in the past few years, especially my own guardian angel, I have begun to regard him (or her) as a friend. Every now and then during the day, walking to work along a noisy and crowded New York avenue or sitting on a bus for longer trips, or in the back seat of a cab en route to LaGuardia Airport, I turn my head and smile and say a silent hello to my angel. And most nights, as I'm falling asleep, I sense his presence next to me or towering above me, and feel comforted and fall asleep in seconds. Of course, I don't see my angel. I don't hear him. I have to imagine him. He is an idea. He is an abstraction, but one that is very much alive in a world that exists beyond my ordinary senses.

And my angel is a friend. Like any good friend, he is there for me, protecting, guiding, enlightening, trustworthy, and generous. Like any good friendship, it's a two-way street. Certainly he doesn't need my guidance and protection. Being an angel, his knowledge is vastly superior to my own. What I am able to give him in return, as his friend, is my faith in his existence, my determination to be the best person I can be—never perfect, surely failing from time to time—and sharing with him in his respect for God and willingness to do His will.

Friendship with God, as I see it, is very similar, only more so. It's a new idea for me. Growing up, I was really afraid of God. I hoped that the promises He had made, which I heard about in church and read in the Bible, were true, promises of peace and contentment, of life beyond life, of green pastures, and something called a beatific vision (being with Him, face to face, forever, and overwhelmed with joy by such a state of being). But I was primarily afraid that I wouldn't make it, that like Ahab, my flesh would be eaten by dogs and my soul would burn in a fiery furnace for all eternity. So I was compulsively good, like a child who walks the pavement carefully to avoid stepping on the cracks.

The next stage in my faith didn't happen until I was about thirty or so, a doctor in practice, married with children. I don't know quite how it happened, maybe it was ignited reading Teihard de Chardin's Phenomenon of Man, in which the Jesuit paleontologist took a hard look at the theory of evolution and postulated that human beings are still caught up in this process, but that it has now assumed more of a psychological and social form—the development of the person and of his or her relationships with others—ultimately leading to what he called the Omega point, by which he meant union with God.

Chardin's thinking influenced my psychiatric and clinical work and set the stage for a new way of viewing certain kinds of mental illness, especially the experience of depression. Suddenly I realized that being depressed was not a disorder in and of itself, but rather it became a sickness when the depressed person, who often had good reason to be depressed, failed to recognize it, master it, and recover from it successfully to become more than he or she had been before—a kind of personal evolution, an opportunity to learn and grow, a period of revelation, a chance to move forward toward a higher degree of wholeness, and, if one's spiritual life were a part of it, holiness as well.

It was a very hopeful vision. But its influence on my own spiritual life was even more significant than that on my professional work. What I came to realize had been there right in front of me all along, but it was as if I were seeing and appreciating it for the first time: God's message of mercy, forgiveness, and love. It was as if I were looking at a different kind of God, no less awesome, no less powerful, but a God who really wanted me to be happy and lead a successful life, and to incorporate within myself and in my behavior toward others the very same gifts that He was offering to me.

But it is only now, in the early winter of my life, that I have begun to see God as literally reaching out His hand to me in friendship, as in Michaelangelo's painting of the Creation of Adam on the ceiling of the Sistine Chapel in Rome. There's God the Father, on the right, portrayed as an elderly man with long white hair and a flowing beard surrounded by angels, reaching his hand out to nearly touch that of the young handsome Adam, whose arm stretches out to nearly touch God.

"To have faith is to stake one's life on God's love," wrote Eugene Joly, "to make God one's center of gravity instead of oneself." God's hand is always out to us. Where are ours? "Faith is an encounter with the living God," Joly goes on, "it means letting God in. An encounter between two persons is always something mysterious and ineffable. And if one of the two persons is God . . . .?"

FAITH AS A WAY OF LIFE

Picture an evangelical healer, standing before a crowd of hundreds of people, shouting at the top of his or her voice: "Where is your hand? Is it reaching out to God? Or is it hanging limply at your side, or is it in your pocket, holding onto your keys or your money clip? Where is it? Where should it be? Put it there, now!" For a few minutes you lift it up into the air and you too feel lifted up and maybe you are "touched by the spirit" and swoon, falling comfortably to the floor.

That's a kind of faith, an excitement of the moment. And perhaps you will be one of the few who are physically healed by the experience.

Maybe it will be the beginning of a new life of faith, a turnaround, what some call conversion. But it's what comes after that really matters.

There is an ongoing life of faith, a sometimes comfortable, sometimes strong, sometimes feeble, life of faith that evolves within one over the years, influencing how one positions everything in one's experience, mingled with fear, awe, the comfort of knowing one is being cared after, offering purpose and passion, and filled with the gratitude and respect one usually has toward a very best friend.

To Lose One's Faith

Few things are more threatening to a religious person than to go through a period in which his or her faith seems to have vanished altogether. Some years ago I treated a minister in his middle forties for a severe depression. The grief that Andrew felt after his wife's untimely death in an automobile accident was compounded by his loss of faith in his vocation, even in God himself. "I feel nothing," he told me. "An emptiness. Confusion. Anger that I've wasted my life being a minister. I thought I had it all. A purpose in life. A great family. The grace of God. But I don't. It's all pointless. I can't tell you how many unhappy people I've counseled, and told them to place their faith in God, that He would see them through to the light. Now I feel like a hypocrite. There's no light, only a dark tunnel, and at the end of it, nothing."

Initially, I approached his therapy in a by-the-book manner. I noted his symptoms of hopelessness, concentration difficulty, waking up terrified in the early hours of the morning, exhaustion, anxiety, even fleeting thoughts of suicide. I took his life history, and examined the stressors that had triggered his depression, particularly his wife's death. I offered cautious reassurance that he would recover, cautious because when a person is depressed, too enthusiastic a promise of healing can provoke the very opposite effect it was meant to induce and make a patient feel even more hopeless than before.

I warned him not to make any final conclusions about anything in his present state of mind, seeing all things "as if through a glass darkly." "This is not the time to judge whether your life has been well spent in the ministry or not. It's not even a time for you to question your faith or wonder why it seems to have failed you. This is a medical job, to get you better, even though you may not think that's possible right now . . . to put what you're experiencing in perspective."

"If there is a God," Andrew said almost inaudibly in his second visit, "he's certainly let me down."

"Maybe not," I replied. "You're here, aren't you?" He made no reply.

The severity of Andrew's depression warranted the use of antidepressants. I started him on sertraline, a selective serotonin reuptake inhibitor. I also gave him fifty mgm. of trazedone, another antidepressant I often use to improve a patient's sleep. He scoffed at the idea that a medicine could affect his condition, but he agreed to cooperate nonetheless. A few days later he felt less anxious and was sleeping a bit better. In several weeks, he appeared brighter and more animated, and admitted to feeling considerably less despairing.

"What was that?" he asked, referring to his recollection of the state of utter despondency that had brought him to me in the first place. "Was I losing my mind?"

"No," I said. "Not at all. You were in a serious depression, obviously triggered by losing your wife. But you might well ask, how come? You've always been a man of faith. You do counseling yourself. You're smart, generous, lead a good life. Why couldn't you handle this on your own?"

"I have no idea," he said.

"Partly because of the kind of person you are. You form very deep attachments. You were strongly attached to your wife, I might even say a little too dependent on her. You were strongly committed to your work. You expected too much of yourself, and of God too. In fact, I think you probably got too much personal gratification out of seeing yourself as God's agent. Your clerical collar became more than a job or a mission; it became who you were and, I suspect, may have even made you feel a bit superior at times. So when things fell apart, your sense of self was shattered in the process."

I could see Andrew was listening very carefully. Then he began to offer me a number of examples from his past that confirmed my interpretations.

I now felt free to speak more directly to the matter of his faith. "You know of St. John of the Cross and what he said about 'the dark night of the soul.' This is your dark night. It may not be the last one you experience, but, in the future, you'll be much better prepared to handle yourself in the face of tragedy, and you'll be much more effective in your pastoral work. When people come to you and tell you they're depressed, you'll be able to let them know that you understand what they're feeling and mean it."

"I still feel shaky," he said. "I mean, I still don't know how much I believe."

"Norman Vincent Peale has an answer for that."

"What's the answer?" he asked.

"Prayer," I said.

17

The Search for Faith

ORMAN VINCENT PEALE SUGGESTS the following
for any of us who are searching for faith or have found our
faith eroding and want to take steps to refresh it:

*The art of having faith may be developed [by] the practice of simple
but habitual prayer and devotional meditation . . . if you will definitely set aside a few minutes, ten or even five—to think about God
and Christ, to confess your sins, to pray for those who have done
wrong against you, and to ask for strength, and if you do this consis-
tently day after day, a true faith will before long begin to send a spiritual health and power through your personality.*

Obviously, to be able to do this, you must decide about the under-
lying question of whether God does or does not exist. If you are convinced he does not, then prayer will seem to you like little more than
a process of meditation. That's not necessarily a bad thing in a purely
humanistic way, like Dr. Herbert Benson's relaxation response, a technique that has been shown to be good for your blood pressure and
your overall state of stress-induced tension. It can often help promote
better feelings about yourself and a more optimistic attitude toward

your future. Of course, you may feel it's a sham, and find yourself more comfortable meditating to a preselected mantra.

If you're not sure about God, you can, if you so choose, engage in conditional prayer. You can reach out your hand, tentatively, as if someone is there to embrace it, and who knows what might come to pass?

THE INVISIBLE GOD

By now it must be obvious that all experiences of faith depend on our ability to interact with Someone we can not see, hear, smell, or touch (unless we happen to be saints). I've always considered this a particular challenge for human beings, that with a smattering of evidence, we should put our hearts and lives in the hands of an invisible Person, Who never speaks directly to us by means of the same vocal and auditory systems that we use to speak to each other. Instead, beyond His personal revelations, we are asked to sense God's presence in our lives and use our imaginations to do the rest.

Ah, there's the rub. Imagination. Is that all that faith in God really involves, a product of our fancy? Like Santa Claus and monsters in the night, the tooth fairy, and the Easter bunny hiding colored eggs for us to find? A mythologic relic? A shared delusion? And all because we are called upon to use our imagination to participate in the experience of faith.

The answer to this query lies in a deeper understanding of the nature of imagination itself. Close your eyes and conjure up a few memories, preferably happy ones, of swimming in the cool ocean, graduation from high school, your first love, your wedding day, the day your first child was born. Pick your own. Now, you have the scene in your mind's eye, complete with sound and Technicolor. What mental processes have you used to do this? Recollection is one, visualization another. What you see and hear is entirely within yourself, unless, of course, you are hallucinating. Is it real? No. It's not real. It happened a long time ago. It's not happening now. The image is real, of course, but the event itself has disappeared in the pages of time.

Because it is in your mind you can change it any way you want. Instead of a sunny day, you can imagine it to have been a cloudy one. If your girlfriend wasn't there, you can put her there, on the beach, wearing a pretty red bathing suit and sunglasses and smiling. That's where you put your imagination to work, changing the details, and immediately putting you in touch with a universal human quality called creativity. The scene as your mind now paints it never existed before and only does so now because you have made it happen.

God is not literally an old man with a long white beard, the way Michaelangelo portrayed him. That was a product of the artist's imagination. Nor do angels have wings, but there they are, hovering around God, on the ceiling of the Sistine Chapel, as He creates the world.

Dr. Jane Goodall has devoted her life to her remarkable study of chimpanzees and to the protection of animals and all of nature from destructive exploitation by *Homo sapiens*. In the introduction to her book, *Reason for Hope*, Dr. Goodall writes of her visit to the cathedral of Notre Dame in Paris in 1974.

> *That moment, a suddenly captured moment of eternity, was perhaps the closest I have ever come to experiencing ecstasy, the ecstasy of the mystic. How could I believe it was the chance gyrations of bits of primeval dust that had led up to that moment in time — the cathedral soaring to the sky; the collective inspiration and faith of those who caused it to be built; the advent of Bach himself; the brain, his brain, that translated truth into music; and the mind that could, as mine did then, comprehend the whole inexorable progression of evolution? Since I cannot believe that this was the result of chance, I have to admit anti-chance. And so I must believe in a guiding power in the universe — in other words, I must believe in God.*

We are endowed with a number of mental qualities, such as memory and intelligence. We've also been gifted with a capacity to think and act creatively. This is not to imply that we can create in the sense of making something out of nothing, the way God created the universe. What we can do is make something quite different out of something that already exists, or discover new insights into the world around us, and into ourselves. Open-mindedness is a requirement for creativity. So too is a willingness to dream. And the ability to juxtapose seemingly contradictory ideas without discomfort. Faith, rather than limiting our vision and narrowing our options, gives us a steadfastness that allows us to wonder about everything, even notions which at first seem to challenge our very faith itself. For example, many people find it hard to believe in a God when they look around and see the injustices, the evils, and the suffering in the world. If there were a God, they argue, why would he allow such terrible things to exist, unless he's a monster of some sort? That's a tough one to sort out. On the one hand we talk about a God who sometimes performs miracles, who responds to our prayers for healing, who has compassion for his creatures. On the other, we watch mesmerized every evening as an endless list of horrors flow by on television network news, from rapes and murders to people being maimed and killed in earthquakes in Turkey or brutally slaughtered in central Africa. Sometimes we feel like calling out: "Will God please step forward and be recognized?"

COMING TO TERMS WITH THE PROBLEM OF EVIL

No one has to be told that a great many terrible things happen in the world, some even to you and to me. Those who never believed in God are only more entrenched in their disbelief because of them. Others abandon what faith they had. Still others become disillusioned in God, embittered, not without faith, but unable to pray and alienated from a relationship they once held dear. What kind of a God would let millions be murdered in concentration camps or in the killing fields of southeast Asia or in Rwanda? What kind of a God would let my daughter, Rickie, spend years in hospitals before discovering that the doctors had been operating with the wrong diagnosis all along?

Who is He to take away your forty-three-year-old husband and leave you a widow with three children to support?

In his book, *When Bad Things Happen to Good People*, Rabbi Harold S. Kushner reminds us that the bad things that happen to good people are often a matter of pure chance. Your plane lands safely in bad weather at Chicago's O'Hare airport, but the next one crashes on the runway and explodes, killing all aboard. Others are the result of inherently natural events. The cells in our bodies grow weaker as we age, and eventually we will become ill and die. Many illnesses result, at least in part, from genetic malformations—Tay-Sachs disease, juvenile diabetes, polycystic kidney disease, perhaps schizophrenia. Kushner himself had a son, Aaron, who suffered with progeria, a condition of rapid aging, who suffered greatly from the changes brought about by the disease and ultimately died at the age of fourteen.

If there is a God, then, why does He let such things go on? Kushner makes the point that God doesn't make these things happen. He doesn't even allow them to occur on a case-by-case basis. Events are only following a natural law of the universe. God created this universe, with all its imperfections. He does admit to the possibility of miracles. "Malignancies mysteriously disappear; incurable patients recover; and baffled doctors credit it to an act of God . . . When miracles occur, and people beat the odds against their survival," he cautions, "we would be well advised to bow our heads in thanks at the presence of a miracle, and not think that our prayers, contributions, or abstentions are what did it." God makes up His own mind about when and where to work miracles.

But in general, God holds to the laws He established for all that exists in the world—laws which, by the way, permit us to have some degree of predictability over our lives. Most important, for most Christians, He will not compromise His gift to us of free will, by means of which we can choose to do His bidding or not. To love or not to love, to forgive or not to forgive, to reach out to Him or ignore Him—the choice is always ours. Know that if and when we turn to God in prayer, He will answer. It just may not be the answer we were after, but it will always be the one we need.

Physical illness, mental illness, and spiritual illness, each has an identity of its own. Millions of people died of smallpox, before Jenner introduced the cow pox vaccine. Many undoubtedly had well-integrated personalities. Many unquestionably were believers in God and His promises, but they died as quickly and as surely as those who did not believe. Many good people have become seriously depressed or worse, and, as a rule, all the faith in the world has neither prevented them from getting depressed nor enabled them to recover on their own. Great souls have been overwhelmed by spiritual crises and have had to turn to other human beings for consolation, understanding, and healing.

Many people believe demons are responsible for much of the world's ills. Dr. Francis MacNutt thinks there are demons; he quotes a highly controversial statement by Pope Paul VI to support his belief. In response to the question "what are the greatest needs of the Church today?" Paul VI answered: " . . . one of the greatest needs is defense from that evil which is called the Devil . . . Evil is not merely a lack of something, but an effective agent, a living, spiritual being, perverted and perverting . . . . It is contrary to the teaching of the Bible . . . to refuse to recognize the existence of such a reality . . . or to explain it as a pseudoreality, a conceptual and fanciful personification of the unknown causes of our misfortunes." Dr MacNutt considers praying from deliverance from such an evil spirit to be critical to healing, if one has first discerned that an illness has been caused by an evil spirit.

In *People of the Lie*, psychiatrist M. Scott Peck gives an account of his own conversion to a belief in the reality of demonic power, which occurred as he watched two exorcisms. Peck wrote:

When the demonic finally spoke clearly in one case, an expression appeared on the patient's face that could be described only as Satanic . . . an incredibly contemptuous grin of utter hostile malevolence . . . The patient suddenly resembled a writhing snake of great strength, viciously attempting to bite the team members. More frightening than the writhing body, however, was the face. The eyes were hooded with lazy reptilian torpor-except when the reptile darted out in attack, at which moment the eyes would open wide with blazing hatred . . . what upset me most was the extraordinary sense of a fifty-million-year-old heaviness I received from this serpentine being . . . Almost all the team members were convinced they were at these times in the presence of something absolutely alien and inhuman. The end of each exorcism was signaled by the departure of this Presence from the patient and the room.

The problem of evil seems closely related to the issue of free will, which God has given to human beings, angels, and demons as well. In a way, this is a dilemma of His own making. He could have made the world a completely safe and happy place, while taking away everybody's freedom in the process. But instead He seems to have chosen to allow people (and angels) to make up their own minds about how they will think and behave, and mete out appropriate rewards or punishments as each situation warrants. Many forms of Christianity encourage one to exercise this free will to combat the demons and work against their destructive effects.

FAITH EMPOWERS CREATIVITY

Faith is not required for creativity, but it does provide the creative mind with a special motivation and coherence to tolerate the often swirling, contradictory, confusing, chaotic torrent of ideas that ultimately lead to a new vision. To the extent that creativity is the process of exchanging an old and obsolete way of viewing something, including ourselves, for a new, better, and more meaningful one, it is the fuel of all therapy. When you come to realize that your selfishness and anger have been ruining your health as well as your relationships and start to replace this with generosity and love, you are right in the middle of the disruptive-reintegrative experience at the heart of meaningful insight. The same is true of all important self-revelations, whether these occur in the course of therapy or in the course of deepening faith.

Personality Types and Faith

I've scoured the libraries and Internet to try to find human traits that relate closely to faith. Naturally I looked at the Myers-Briggs Test, based on Carl Jung's theory of personality types. I could not find any good study that explored faith by mean of this instrument. But I've had enough experience in psychiatry to speculate as to what the findings might be.

Here's what the test can reveal. You may be primarily an extrovert, in which case you tend to focus on and derive much of your stimulation from the world of people and things around you. Or you may be primarily an introvert, tending to focus on your own perceptions and ideas, and obtaining most of your stimulation from within yourself.

Each of these broad categories is then broken down into three pairs of opposites. First, sensing is opposed to intuition. Sensate people tend to focus on the here and now and on concrete information gained from their senses; a "what you see is what you get" point of view. Intuitiveness, on the other hand, is associated with focusing on the future, on possibilities, the stuff that dreams are made of.

The next category pits *thinking* against *feeling*. Thinking people base their decisions on logic and an objective analysis of cause and effect. They are dispassionate in their approach to understanding. In contrast, feeling people tend to base their decisions primarily on values (people matter, the environment matters, love matters) and on subjective evaluation of person-centered concerns.

Finally, people who prefer *judgment* tend to like a planned and organized approach to life. In the old days—before the age of mergers and downsizing—these people liked the security of working for companies like American Telephone, Consolidated Edison, or the Pennsylvania Railroad. Perception, on the other hand, is an indicator of people who prefer a more flexible and spontaneous approach to life.

Faith is probably as much an attribute of the *extrovert* as the *introvert*, although the former may be more likely to express it by attendance at religious services and the latter by solitary prayer.

It's easy to see how *intuitive* people can embrace faith, sensing God's presence, not being so imprisoned by a stern logic that demands scientific proof.

It's the *sensate* ones who, I think, might have a special problem with faith. I can't see them having much patience with prayers whispered to Someone no one can see or hear. Miracles? Impossible! (Unless they have a unique opportunity for faith, such as that given to Thomas when the risen Christ reached out his hands for his doubting apostle to touch, to prove that he was really there. "Blessed are they who have not seen and believe," Jesus says.)

The *thinking* type of person can easily become agnostic, unless he or she can form an argument for God's existence that appeals to reason. Feeling people are perhaps the most likely to follow the precepts of faith—loving their neighbors as themselves—but they can do so because they are believers or just because that's the way they're put together.

Finally, people who are characterized by *judgment* are said to like to have things settled. They would seem to be excellent candidates for organized religion, a community of faith, with clear-cut expectations and definite guidelines.

People who prefer *perception* like to keep their options open. It seems to me that how much faith such a person might have would be strongly influenced by his or her priority of values. Perceptive people might keep faith a constant, and strike off in different directions with other aspects of their lives—jobs, boyfriends, girlfriends, hobbies, sports interests, music, movies, travel. But if they apply their preference for flexibility to the experience of faith, I could see them going from one religious structure to another or shifting back and forth between a loosely knit spiritual community and none at all.

This personality typology is not written in stone. All of us possess all of these characteristics, with some being highly developed while others lie dormant. Jung himself described the mid-life crisis of many people to be centered around conflicts between dominant personality styles and potentials that have been largely ignored or suppressed up until this point in their lives. As he saw it, a major goal of therapy was to actualize and cultivate the "other side" of one's makeup; for example, for the very masculine person to recognize and appreciate his more traditionally "feminine" perceptual traits, such as intuition and feeling.

The more we understand ourselves, the more we can see how our personalities affect our experience of faith. The way we perceive the world may interfere with our ability to believe in anything. Or perhaps we can believe only in what we can comprehend with our senses, and our faith rests squarely on a future that scientific discovery will hopefully provide. Maybe you wish you had faith in something or Someone more than mere matter; working to develop your hidden strengths can help you in your search. Maybe you already believe and you want to enrich your faith—for example, it's largely intellectual and you want it to be more an experience of feeling—then you can look for ways to ignite those latent qualities that will make this possible. It seems to me that the fullest faith is to be realized by the personality that is most richly integrated, and the pursuit of such wholeness is a life-long journey.

A psychologist whose chief area of study was visual perception once explained to me that as people migrated from farms to cities, where they were surrounded by massive skyscrapers that obscured the heavens, their perceptual style became ever less vertical (looking up and down) and ever more horizontal (looking straight ahead). Vision is the primary route whereby external stimuli reach our brains. It suddenly occured to me that we may have come upon yet another reason why modern man is having such trouble with spirituality. We can't look in God's direction any more, but only at glass towers, slabs of concrete, neon signs, and our own images reflected in store windows as we walk the pavement, no earth beneath our feet.

18

Overcoming Helplessness

WHY IS IT THAT PEOPLE of faith seem to do better when it comes to recovering from or living with successful resignation to illness? This seems particularly true for those whose faith rests in a personal God, and when their faith is comingled with the recognition that God more often acts through natural means than by means of miracles.

There is a very reasonable and natural effect of faith that partially can explain this. By surrendering ourselves to God's will, faith frees us of the futile need to control the uncontrollable forces that act upon us in our lives. This may not protect us from getting upset, frightened, or even depressed, when such reactions are clearly warranted. But by offering us profound reassurance, faith can ease our way and counteract the destructive physical and psychological effects that any state of prolonged helplessness is likely to induce.

PHYSICAL COMPLICATIONS OF HELPLESSNESS

Numerous laboratory studies with animals have presented us with compelling evidence of the link between stress—or rather how stress is managed—and our bodies. For example, one study involving laboratory animals explored the endocrine, immune, and sympathetic nervous system responses to several different stressful situations. When the subjects were prevented from dealing effectively with the stress, a decrease in cytokine interleukin-6 production, and increased levels of cortisol occurred. However, when these animals were able, through effort, to reduce the stressful stimuli, immunological processes and natural killer cell (NK) activity were enhanced. In another study, animals were exposed to electric shock stimuli; the degree of control they could exert over the shock was inversely related to ACTH and cortisone levels.

In another study, this time involving human subjects, sudden, acute stress induced increased circulation concentrations of epinephrine, norepinephrine, beta-endorphin, adrenocorticotropic hormone (ACTH), and cortisol, along with a selective redistribution of natural killer (NK) cells into the peripheral blood, whereas those subjects who had been *chronically* stressed beforehand showed even higher peaks of epinephrine, lower peak levels of beta-endorphin and of NK cell lysis, and a more pronounced redistribution of NK cells in response to the acute stress. The acute stressor also induced a protracted decline in NK lysis per NK cell in this group. We can conclude from this experiment that when a person who is undergoing chronic life stresses is confronted with an *acute* psychological challenge, an exaggerated reactivity occurs, associated with decrements in individual NK cell function, an effect which extends well beyond termination of the stressor. In other words, the less control and the greater the helplessness, the greater the physical damage occuring as a result of stress.

In ordinary language, studies such as these confirm the fact that it's not just the stresses we encounter that cause us grief; it's *how we respond to them*, and especially whether we feel helpless to do anything about them and for how long. Too much cortisol production over too long a period of time can lead to exhaustion, depletion of calcium from bone, and other forms of tissue damage. Decreased NK cell function reduces the immune system's ability to do its job protecting the body against the onslaught of infectious and toxic agents.

PERSONALITY TYPES, HELPLESSNESS, AND SUSCEPTIBILITY TO DISEASE

Drs. Ronald Grossarth-Maticek and H. J. Eysenck have described the close relationship that exists between personality type and vulnerability to heart disease and cancer. Moreover, these connections are far more significant than the already well-known and accepted ones between smoking or cholesterol levels and these diseases. That is not to imply that other factors, including diet, vitamin supplementation, and exercise are not important determinants, but rather that how we experience what we experience may be the most powerful of them all.

The psychosomatic approach to understanding disease is hardly new. The public knows about this, although many people may not really understand it or appreciate how important it is to their health. We still live in a culture in which psychological and behavioral problems are much more embarrassing to admit to than a wide variety of physical ailments. The type-A and type-B personality types—type-A being more prone to heart disease than type-B—is common knowledge today. However, this concept has been revised in the twenty years since its original formulation. Only certain aspects of type-A behavior have held up to scrutiny as being predictive of coronary heart disease, namely persistent or frequent anger, aggression, and hostility.

The influence of the mind on the body was a new area for study when I was a medical student many years ago. I can still recall my professor, Harold Wolff, a world-renowned neurologist, bringing his patient named Tom into the lecture hall. Tom had suffered a gunshot wound to his abdomen and it had never entirely healed. As a consequence, a small amount of pale pink stomach lining protruded for all to see. Dr. Wolff whispered something that frustrated Tom, and instantaneously the tissue turned bright red. We stared in amazement. In those days, stress was thought to make a major contribution to ulcer formation. What we saw happen to Tom served to make us certain of that. (The idea that a bacterial infection was the real culprit and that ulcers would be treated with antibiotics was still four decades away.)

Hippocrates was certainly ahead of his time when he dared to suggest that melancholy constituted an essential personality antecedant to cancer. Only in the past few years have careful studies demonstrated that men and women who suffer with persistent depression—usually because they haven't been adequately treated for it—have a greater vulnerability to disease, which only makes sense when you consider that the immune systems in depressed people are also seriously compromised.

But Grossarth-Maticek and Eysenck get much more specific. Their studies reveal four types of personalities that appear to be associated with health or illness. Type 1 has an increased risk of cancer mortality. These people manifest strong needs to be close to another person emotionally, or to pursue and achieve some highly valued goal. However, the object of their need or pursuit has permanently withdrawn. It is beyond their reach, in spite of which they still consider it essential for their happiness and well-being. They may try to find something to replace it or to divorce themselves from it, but these efforts fail. Because they can never have whatever they have been after, they feel worthless, hopeless, depressed, and helpless—an assortment of physically dangerous feelings that they try their best to conceal, even from themselves.

Type 2 has an increased vulnerability to dying of a heart attack or stroke. Type 2 people show an intense need to distance themselves from disturbing persons or situations. But they can't. This results in an ongoing state of irritation and anger, a feeling of being trapped, and again, helplessness.

Type 3 has an average, or even a better than average survival rate. They seem to be people with conflicting desires. They want closeness, but they're afraid of it. They are very dependent on others (or on conditions) about whom they feel very mixed, and although they may experience anxiety or episodes of aggressiveness, they are not depressed and do not feel the helplessness so characteristic of types 1 and 2. This doesn't strike me as a very happy state of affairs. Type 3 people may often seek psychiatric help for their emotional and interpersonal difficulties, but they do not appear to be at increased risk of physical disease.

Type 4 people actually enjoy an increased survival rate. They have a healthy sense of self-confidence and autonomy, and they regard others as having the right to be the same way. They are in touch with their emotions and know how to express them effectively. They like themselves. They like other people. They learn from experience. When anything happens to compromise their self-esteem, they are able to regain it in short order. They handle their relationships with others easily, knowing how to trust and bringing a generosity of spirit to each occasion. They are what all of us wish we could be.

The findings of Grossarth-Maticek and Eysenck are impressive. But all they had, at this point, were a series of highly suspicious correlations, the same kind of correlations that link cigarrette smoking to cancer and high cholesterol levels to heart disease. It was premature to draw the conclusion of a direct causal relationship between personality types and illness.

So they took another step. They took 100 cancer-prone and ninety-two heart disease-prone individuals (types 1 and 2) and divided them into two equal-sized groups. One group, called the control group, was left alone. The other group participated in a program of individual therapy lasting a total of twenty-five to thirty hours. An effort was made to change the subjects in type 1 or type 2 to move toward a more type 4 profile, by encouraging greater autonomy, a less constricted attitude toward emotional recognition and expression, and, most of all, better coping mechanisms to deal with the interpersonal stress to replace the inadequacies so prominent in both types.

Individuals in both the control group and those who received treatment were followed for thirteen years. At the end of that time, only nineteen (38%) of the untreated cancer-prone group were still living, in contrast to forty-five (90%) in the therapy group; sixteen (32%) of the control subjects had died specifically of cancer, whereas none of the treated subjects had.

Similar results were seen in the heart infarct/stroke group: only seventeen (36.9%) in the control group were still alive versus thirty-seven (89.4%) in the treated group; sixteen (34.7%) of the untreated control subjects had died specifically of heart attacks/strokes, whereas only three (6.5%) of the treated group had.

The level of significance is astounding. The implications are more astounding. But, to a physician, they are hardly surprising. The common denominator in subjects who received treatment was the restoration of a sense of command over the conditions of their lives, reducing the hopelessness and helplessness that had dogged them for so long and taken such a toll on their bodies.

Wow! If it's that easy, show me the way to the nearest behavioral therapist, you might think. Or better yet, we already believe in ourselves. We get along with the people in our lives pretty well. We don't want anything we can't possibly attain, and we can get out of any relationship or situation that demoralizes us. We'll live forever, especially now that we work out regularly, take dietary supplements, do breathing exercises every night, and stop to meditate whenever the going gets rough. Well, maybe not forever.

What's usually missing in reports of this kind research is the kind of detailed information about the people involved that would let us really get to understand them. Specifics of what actually happens in the therapeutic sessions are also not reported, as well as the character and skills of the therapists themselves. Common sense tells us that if you have better coping skills, you will be less likely to feel helpless or get into predicaments that might cause you to feel helpless. It's safe to assume that the treated patients gained a certain level of faith—although faith isn't mentioned as such—and if they did, we still don't know in what or whom they believed. Could similar results have been obtained if these subjects had been directed to participate in twenty-five hours of prayer?

CONTEMPORARY IDOLATRY

It's possible to postulate that type 1, the person so needy of a relationship or an achievement he can never have, suffers with a common malady called idolatry. James W. Fowler defines contemporary idolatry as "the profoundly serious business of committing oneself or betting one's life on finite centers of value and power as the source of one's confirmation of worth and meaning, and as the guarantor of survival with quality." Even if one has the outward trappings of religious faith—in contrast to intrinsic faith—his or her hierarchy of values may not place faith in God and surrender to His will at the top of his list of priorities. Worshipping in the temple of Baal is not likely to be commonplace today, except in Indiana Jones films. Other idols— rock groups, movie stars, wealth, corporate power, sex, activities, politicians, even active participation in very worthwhile enterprises such as education or refugee relief—may be more valued than one's relationship with God. One of my grown children suggested that hundreds of years into the future, archeologists may uncover the ruins of Disney World, and hypothesize that in the late part of the twentieth century human beings reverted to a form of paganism and worshipped a mouse. Yet, all these idols, being earthbound, are capable of generating severe frustration and disappointment, providing, in the end, a spiritual emptiness that renders us more susceptible to disease.

Michael Kimmelman, in a *New York Times* article called "How Photography Makes Celebrity So Irresistible," makes the connection between the discovery and exploitation of the camera and a new kind of fame. " . . . fame stripped of its everlasting value, its promise of a life after death, at least for one's reputation, has lost its spiritual underpinning. Historically speaking, it used to be a spiritual matter, and it retains certain aspects of its spiritual character while no longer necessarily attaching itself to the ultimate spiritual goal, eternal existence.

"Hence the vocabulary of fame still borrows from religion: charisma, idol. We still collect and revere pictures of the famous as if they were icons, whether they're baseball cards or rock star posters. And what is an endorsement, in the end, but the sanctioning of something by the sanctified, the famous person lending his or her aura to a product?"

When the dilemmas faced by people in type 2—their inability to escape damaging relationships and circumstances—are combined with the with anger and hostility characteristic of the type-A personality, there must be an even greater risk of dying of cardiovascular disease. Whatever faith such a person may have, it would not seem to have translated itself into the gifts that should accompany it, such as the ability to let go of hatred and to forgive.

Being too sensitive to rejection can also keep you in unrewarding and potentially damaging relationships. Too often the person or situation you realize you must get away from plays games with your need for acceptance. By means of an on-again, off-again behavior pattern that tells you you are loved and appreciated one day and deprecates you the next, a boyfriend, girlfriend, husband, wife, or boss can cripple your self-esteem and paralyze your ability to make decisions.

What we all need are genuinely consistent, trustworthy, resilient, loving relationships. We can surely find these with good people. But there's only one place you can hope to find a love that is truly complete and unwavering, and that's in the heart of God.

19

Physical and Psychological Resilience

*A*S THE PREVIOUS CHAPTER discussed, our attitudes and behavior influence our mental and physical health. What is much more complicated to grasp is the relationship between the mental and emotional selves, which is called our psyche, and our spiritual selves, our immaterial, transcendental, immortal souls.

It's not easy to distinguish the psyche from the soul, as closely fused as they are during our earthly existence. This is made even more problematic by authors and lecturers who speak to us about soul, but who are really offering us sage advice that relates mostly to our psyches. Becoming more assertive, achieving a comfortable appreciation of your talents and strengths, building self-confidence, mastering the art of forgiveness, being a more loving and giving person, all are invaluable lessons to learn. But your spiritual life is much more than a set of healthy emotional responses. It begins with the faith that, even though we are animals, something within us is intangible, supernatural, eternal, more valuable than anything else we possess, and it is that part of ourselves that ties us most closely with a largely unseen God.

Here on earth, mind, body, and spirit are all rolled into one. How healthy any one of these is depends, in significant measure, on how well all three are functioning, in and of themselves, and in relation to each other.

A Sound Mind and Soul in a Sound Body

There are many common-sense tactics that we can employ to achieve good physical health. Having regular checkups with your doctor is one. Exercise is another. Exercise has been shown to reduce the risk of heart disease and osteoporosis. It also serves to give us greater strength and endurance which help us to minimize our risk of accidents, especially that of falling down, which can carry with it numerous less and more serious consequences. Exercise also helps us control our weight, another factor contributing to our health. Healthy sleep habits. No smoking. Cautious use of alcohol. Careful driving. Good nutrition. Advice we've heard from healing experts a thousand times or more.

Jean Carper is the author of *Miracle Cures*, in which she joins the ranks of numerous nutritionists who hold out hope that what we eat and drink will significantly affect our health and longevity. I guess she used the word "miracle" in her title because most of these remedies involve natural "God-produced" substances rather than pharmaceuticals. So-called alternative treatments were disdained by the Western medical profession for years, but with the popularity of writers and lecturers like Dr. Andrew Weil, physicians now must assume that most of their patients pay close attention to dietary supplementation and follow the news about natural healing on television, in newspapers and their favorite magazines, and nowadays on the Internet as well. Doctors are becoming more familiar with the subject so as to understand what their patients are up to, offer intelligent opinions, and at least be open-minded to the possibilities of methods of prevention and treatment that do not use officially sanctioned medications. Medicine's request for studies to document the effects and risks of herbal therapies is very reasonable, but money, skill, and willingness to perform them have been slow to emerge.

My own physician has me taking a variety of vitamins and I take a few more on my own. But doing so has not deterred me from taking appropriate antibiotics when I have a serious infection, like bronchitis (after consultation with my doctor of course). I have as much reluctance to take pharmaceuticals as the next person. But whether a curative substance grows on a bush or is synthesized in a laboratory, to me it's still a manifestation of God's able hand. His part in its creation is equally apparent.

A Sound Body and Soul in a Sound Mind

Psychobiological resilience is the key to a healthy psyche. Some years ago I defined what I call the resilience hypothesis. According to this construct, change and the stress that accompanies change must disrupt whatever equilibrium we have established for ourselves in order for a new, better, more effective equilibrium to take its place. This process applies to the minutiae of life as well as its great moments.

For example, someone you care a lot about gets angry at you. Perhaps his outburst was triggered by something you did, or failed to do. Or perhaps he's just tense and out of sorts. Your feelings are hurt. You may shout back. Or you may stifle your reaction and settle into a profound silence. You may feel guilty. You may feel outraged. You may feel numb. In any event, your previous equilibrium has been shattered, a little or a lot, and the comfort one usually feels in a state of equilibrium vanishes.

What's your next move? If you were in the wrong, you could apologize and hope to be forgiven. If not, you could defend yourself, protesting, attacking in return. Or you could brood, and let your own anger solidify into resentment. Or you could step aside mentally and emotionally, try to figure out where the other person is coming from, and, without placating, even without words, let him or her realize that your feelings of respect and affection are still there.

The choice is yours. But however it turns out, nothing between you can ever be quite the same again. A new equilibrium emerges, within you and between the two of you. The relationship may be slightly wounded. Or, through understanding and forgiveness, it can be much stronger than it was before.

GREAT MOMENTS IN THE LIFE CYCLE

Throughout our lives, we experience changes, some bigger than others, some monumental. Many of these changes are tied into the cycle of life itself, from birth to death. Being born is a big change. The first few years of every child's life is filled with change as he or she goes through the ordinary stages of mental and physical development. (If you're not familiar with these stages, you might read Piaget or Erickson, or, a good deal easier, Spock or Brazelton.)

Starting school is a change. So are puberty, graduation, getting a first job, falling in and out of love, getting married, having children, getting divorced, reaching middle age and finding your home empty of children, retiring, losing your hair or watching it turn gray, noticing lines in your face that weren't there before, and, for women, menopause. It doesn't stop there. There's a gradual decline in sexual desire and performance. Family and friends start to look really old and, one by one, they begin to die off. Things you used to do with ease tire you out. Aches and pains that weren't there before besiege you. Serious illness. Your own dying.

Then there are the unexpected changes: automobile accidents, financial reverses, homes burning down, children not growing up the way you'd hoped they would, children dying, ovarian cancer at thirty, a heart attack at forty-two, widowhood at fifty.

Every change is stressful, have no doubt about it! Of course, how stressful depends on what the change is, how suddenly it happens, how long it goes on. *The effect it has on you depends greatly on how prepared you are to meet and deal with it.* Will you be able to go through the nightmare of divorce and come out on the other side of the anguish and bewilderment to build a new life? Or will you stew for years, feeling like a failure, guilty, rejected, unable to trust, bitter, one more victim of crumbling faith?

READINESS IS ALL

Readiness is all, said Hamlet. To be ready you must know that the stress of change is, by its very nature, disruptive. It not only affects our psyches; it also affects our bodies and our souls, producing a disharmony that persists until we are able to put the pieces of ourselves and our lives together again to form a new whole.

Being in a state of disequilibrium is uncomfortable at best, and in its most extreme form, frightening, depressing, and interlaced with profound helplessness. Only by being resilient can its potentially devasting consequences be avoided. Many men and women who turn to me for professional help are caught in this sort of immobilization, not "mentally ill" in the true sense of the term, but unable to create a new equilibrium on their own.

FAILING TO FALL APART

The people who seek the help of friends or professionals at times of crises are the lucky ones. They avoid the trap of denial. Neither do they refuse to accept that a significant change has taken place nor do they block out their emotional responses to it. Those who do will not only fail to learn and grow as a result of their predicament; they also risk a decline in their physical health. I know of more than one instance of young men in their forties, working and living under great stress, who cannot allow themselves to appreciate the emotional turmoil inside themselves, much less deal with it appropriately, who suddenly drop dead in the middle of a game of tennis.

The first rule for successfully transitting the disruption-reintegration cycle is to accept that stress and change bring with them episodes of disequilibrium, disruption, and emotional distress in the natural course of things, and that this is *a necessary prelude to the healing to follow.*

TOTAL COLLAPSE

For a variety of reasons, some people lose it altogether. They don't just get apprehensive because they think they might be demoted at work; they panic. They don't just get sad and discouraged because they've lost money in the stock market or their spouses have been giving them a hard time; they become absolutely overwhelmed with hurt, suffering, and self-deprecation.

Sometimes the cause of this is physical. The biochemical changes that always accompany emotional upheavals are not operating effectively. They aren't sufficiently self-limiting, and the nervous system just gets out of hand. Lack of exercise, poor health habits, inadequate nutrition, and faulty genes all make a contribution. Sometimes it's because there's no one to turn to or confide in and from whom to gain solace and empathy. Often it is because they don't possess enough personal resilience.

The second rule for managing the disruption induced by change is to be prepared by being in the best mental and physical condition you can be. Have at least one good friend and confidant to whom you can reach out. If you need professional help, get it. And put your faith in God. Pray to Him for strength and guidance to see it through.

PUTTING THE PIECES TOGETHER AGAIN

The most frequent complication of any stressful experience is to never fully recover from its impact. Instead of creating a new, wiser, stronger self and achieving greater harmony with everything and everyone in your life, your reintegration remains incomplete. Emotional distress—helplessness, anxiety, depression, confusion, distrust, resentment, lack of self-confidence, lack of faith—lingers on in a chronically disabling form.

The third rule for successfully weathering this cycle of disruption and reintegration is to take advantage of this unique opportunity to learn all you can about yourself so you can become a better person, better prepared to face the challenges and opportunities that lie in your future.

How well you do at this will depend on how resilient a person you are, the operational integrity of your physiological systems, and the quality of your relationships with the people around you, as well as with God.

Becoming a More Resilient Person

I've discussed the essentials of personal resilience in my book *Resilience*. There's so much to say about it, I can't really do justice to the subject here. But I can highlight a few of the cardinal principles. Here are some guidelines.

- *Know how to hold onto your self-esteem and to restore it when its been battered.* A failed marriage, for example, or a failed career are two obvious assaults to one's self-esteem. Counterbalance this pain by looking back into your past, remembering the good and generous things you did. Recall your successes in school and at work. Reach out to those whom you love who love you. Include God in that. Recognize and get rid of any embarrassment or humiliation you may feel, since these can easily serve as straightjackets, delaying or blocking altogether your recovery.

- *Reexamine the sources of your personal worth.* Most of us have several. Which ones matter most depend on the value we place on them. For example, my own self-esteem would be compromised if I felt I weren't a good husband and father or an effective physician. I'd also feel less of myself if I thought I'd lost my ability to communicate. I wouldn't know how to react if I thought I'd lost my faith in God. One friend of mine's self-esteem goes up and down with the movements of the stock market. Another's soars or plummets depending on how she sees herself in her mirror. Yet another's are clearly correlated with how many important people she can get to come to her elegant summer dinner parties, like Hyacinth on the British television comedy, Keeping Up Appearances. Faithful people can find their sense of worth in their humanity, that is—to quote the child's catechism—to believe that humans are made in the image and likeness of God, meant to serve Him in this world and be happy with Him in the next. A very consoling thought indeed.

• *Independence of thought and action.* Developing self-reliance is an ongoing process. It begins with the small child's first mastery of crawling, standing up, walking, learning to speak and read and comprehend, and continues until a relatively integrated self is established. Now we are able to exercise our free will in most situations, draw our own conclusions about God and faith, and stand our ground for what we believe in. We can take care of ourselves. We can do the same for those who depend on us.

• *Know how to depend on others.* None of us entirely loses the need to depend on other people. That's what lovers and friends are for. Professionally, I encounter as many people who deny such a need as I do those who suffer from too much dependency. They think they can do just about everything all by themselves and are afraid to rely on anyone else, least of all for emotional support. Knowing how to rely on others increases our ability to rely on ourselves. I recall one forty-plus woman who came to see me—I'm still not sure why. During our one and only consultation she was so resistant to accepting her need for help that she wouldn't even sit down. Throughout the session, which lasted only fifteen minutes, she stood, occasionally walking around the room and pausing to speak, several times making the point that she didn't trust anybody enough to reveal herself to him, and then, handing me a check, took her leave. There is always a risk in placing your faith in another person, but this is a risk we must be willing to take, in order to survive and to be happy. If you place your trust wisely and well, you'll seldom be disappointed. But if you're looking for someone who's always reliable, add God to your list.

• *Develop a high level of personal discipline and a sense of responsibility.* Creative and successful people in any field aren't flakes. They're people who get the job done in a timely and workmanlike way. They prepare themselves for eventualities. They prepare themselves for their work. They put in the time and effort to learn to be resilient.

• *Play from your strengths.* How often have you heard that advice? Too often. But have you stopped to make a list of your own strengths and weaknesses, your talents, the things that come naturally and those that take considerable effort and the ones you never seem able to master? If you're lucky, you can play the piano. Or at least, you took piano lessons when you were young. A recent study indicated that youngsters who were given piano lessons ended up more than 30% more able to deal with abstract concepts than those who did not, including youngsters who had been schooled in computer skills. I never kept up with my piano playing, but I'm grateful I was exposed to music at an early age, because I'm sure it helped me with my talent for language. Some people are natural athletes. Others are born salespersons. Still others are gifted laboratory researchers. A good healer is inherently empathic. A good surgeon is accomplished with his or her hands. Someone who has been given a gift of strong faith can not only rely on it during trying times, but he or she can quietly share it with others in hopes that they may be inspired by it to find a faith of their own. A friend of mine once told me that she was never really sure about her faith in God, even though she attended services every week. But as she came to know what faith meant to me, her own became more meaningful to her. "If someone like you, a psychiatrist, a scientist, can believe, there has to be something to it," she said.

• *Recognize and accept your limitations.* Some limitations are insurmountable. If you can't catch a baseball, there's not much chance of making the varsity team. If you're terrible with numbers, don't think of becoming an accountant. If you aren't dexterous, give up your dream of being a brain surgeon, as I had to do. However, sometimes you can work hard to overcome or compensate for limitations, like Demosthenes who, suffering with a speech impediment, practiced uttering words with a mouth full of pebbles, and went on to be one of the greatest orators of ancient Greece. If you have difficulty expressing yourself, you might take a course in *How to Win Friends and Influence People at Dale Carnegie*, or go for assertiveness training. If you're chronically late, you can make every effort to be more timely. If you have trouble setting limits on the behavior of others, stop to take a look at who in your life has been taking advantage of you because of this imperfection and start to put your foot down, firmly or diplomatically as the case requires.

• *Have an open mind and be intelligently receptive to new ideas, which you can appraise and accept or reject later, as good judgment indicates.* Fresh input is bound to stimulate your mind and imagination, and help you achieve new and valuable perspectives. You can discover new insights into yourself and others. You can learn new ways to do just about everything, from cooking to traveling to buying a car or a home, from growing flowers to enjoying good music to reading exciting authors you've never read before. The processing of new information by the open mind is not obstructed by powerful convictions and biases that afflict so many of us. Concepts that challenge what you already feel sure about are going to invade your brain one way or another, and it's best that they do so while you're awake and can know what's going on than when you're blind, and they're left to penetrate into your subconscious where they can cause quite a bit of trouble.

• *Be creative and resourceful.* Being observant and open to new ideas is only the first step in becoming more creative in your thoughts and actions. Learn to refrain from premature closure and knee-jerk criticism of concepts and suggestions from others, as well as those that arise from within yourself. Coming up with a long list of thoughts in search of solutions to any problem is far more likely to lead you to one that is superior and that actually works than settling for the first one that comes to mind; by brainstorming, you try to tap the power of your subconscious mind, where more original and imaginative thoughts reside and where seemingly contradictory notions can be combined to form new images, beyond the strict constraints of logic and reason. That's why simmering, putting your search aside for a little while to allow the subconscious energies to work on it, is often so necessary to the creative process. Evaluating your new options comes in later on, as you assess their value in the cold light of day and test them in the real world.

• *Use your creativity to facilitate healing of the psyche.* Art therapy and psychodrama can be extremely helpful to patients suffering with various mental disorders. But it's not painting a picture or playing a role that really makes the difference. In its broad sense, creativity applies to every aspect of life. It involves making something new, different, better than what came before. Some psychologists refer to the product of creativity as a new gestalt, a new whole, a new way of looking at yourself, a new way to view the world around you. And that is precisely what healing of the psyche entails. It's quite different from healing the body. When your body has been insulted by disease or damaged by injury, your primary goal is to get it back to where it was before. (There are some exceptions, as in the case of infectious diseases, like measles or mumps, which leave you with an immunity to future assaults.) You want your broken arm or ulcerated stomach to function as close to the way it used to as possible. If your disease cannot be entirely reversed you may have to take supplements to help your body function as it once did, like insulin for diabetes or thyroid hormone for hypothyroidism. This return to the status quo is not the goal of psychological recovery. Because of what you have been through—the death of someone close to you or a disruption in your personal life, such as a divorce or losing your job, and the emotional turbulence and depression that accompanies it—you will never be the same again. Nor should you be. The experience itself and what gave rise to it are enough to change you. More important, this is your chance to discover something about yourself, change old attitudes and behaviors that have been detrimental to your success and well-being, and create a new identity. You're still the same person, of course, but with greater strength and skill to master the opportunities and vicissitudes of your present and future life. Being overwhelmed by the loss of someone upon whom you were excessively dependent can set the stage for appreciating and developing a higher degree of personal autonomy and self-reliance. The collapse of a marriage can be the fertile soil for you to understand and implement the gifts of love, compassion, and forgiveness, with which you may have been previously quite inept.

• *Hold onto your sense of humor. In the 1940s movie,* Singing in the Rain, *Donald O'Connor performs a delightful number called "Make 'Em Laugh."* If you're feeling down in spirit, watch this film. If you're not too depressed, it's practically guaranteed to make you feel better. It's a healing film. Norman Cousins, in his book *Anatomy of an Illness,* makes a strong case for the value of films and humor as catalysts for recovery from illness. In 1990, several years before he died, my daughter Rickie and I had the chance of spending an hour with this sensitive and caring man, in his office at the University of California School of Medicine in Los Angeles. He asked what Rickie thought had enabled her to survive so many years of suffering and come out of it so well. She replied: "Faith. Prayer. A wonderful family. My dad's willingness to take me out of the medical system, which had failed in my case, and get me into rehab, and get my vision fixed, and a nutritional program . . . things that doctors used to look down on." She smiled.

"And a sense of humor," she said, knowing of his special regard for the healing power of humor. "You could say that when everything wasn't totally black, I could look at what I was going through and see the absurdity of it and laugh, at my predicament, at all the funny situations that happen every day, even in a hospital for the mentally ill."

• *Know how to really love and sustain meaningful human relationships.* We know we're supposed to love our neighbor as we do ourselves, in the agape sense of love. But most of us are limited in our ability to really love by the belief that some people are more neighborly than others, and some aren't our neighbors at all. A heart-felt recognition that everyone is our neighbor is possible only for the truly creative mind that can distinguish between the humanity of every person and his or her specific personality characteristics. It's what enables us to rid ourselves of racial and religious bigotry and relate to others for who they are, one by one. We don't have to like everyone. We just have to love them.

• *Cherish your faith, your commitment to life, the philosophical framework within which you can interpret personal experiences with meaning and hope, even at your most hopeless moments.* As I wrote in the final pages of my book on resilience, "From prisoner of war camps to divorce courts, from the hospital bedside of someone you love who is dying to the playing fields where you reach out breathlessly for the will to win, I believe the most vital ingredient of resilience is faith. For some, faith will exist within the framework of formal religion; for others, it lies in the deepest level of our unconscious minds in touch with eternal truths." This is where our psyches and our spiritual selves truly meet and fuse with one another.

20

*Spiritual Resilience:
Healing the Soul*

THESE PRINCIPLES OF RESILIENCE apply no less to our spiritual lives than they do to our psychological ones.

- A strong and supple sense of one's own spiritual worth.
- Self-reliance, a quality of great religious leaders, martyrs, and saints, to help us stand firmly against any and all attacks on our spirit and to strengthen our free will in the pursuit of good.
- Healthy dependency on other people, especially a network of friends who are supportive of one's spiritual life; genuine, complete acknowledgment of one's dependency on God.
- The regular exercise of love and generosity, enabling us to fulfill the commandment to love others as we love ourselves.
- A high level of discipline and a sense of responsibility, useful for following God's commandments, and for prayer.
- Recognition of and gratitude for one's spiritual gifts, with an intelligent appreciation of one's spiritual weaknesses and the desire to overcome them.

- A creative mind that is open to the possibilities of spiritual enrichment.
- A sense of humor that can even be directed at one's relationship with God.
- Being committed to the life of the spirit, with a solid world view through which to interpret all that happens in our lives.

A SPIRITUAL LIFE CYCLE

Childhood. Our spiritual lives have their own life cycles. Even as the psychological and interpersonal quality of childhood contributes to the evolution of our personal strengths, so too does the spirituality of the environment in which we grow up significantly affect how well-formed and meaningful our spiritual vitality will be. Too harsh a religious exposure can rob us of joy that should be part of our being; it can turn us off to religion for years, perhaps for the rest of our lives. Since children tend to model their thinking after that of their parents, I often wonder what kind of faith well meaning fathers and mothers expect their youngsters to develop if they themselves demonstrate no signs of faith themselves. "Let Billy and Sally decide for themselves about God when they're older without any guidance from us" is a little like saying "They can decide for themselves whether they consider education of any value, without any undue encouragement from us."

Adolescence. For many youngsters, adolescence represents a challenge to whatever faith and spirituality they may have learned at home. As they move toward greater independence, sometimes smoothly, sometimes struggling to do so, they are especially vulnerable to the values of their peers. Obviously, the boys and girls of Littleton, Colorado were part of a more or less God-centered community; they accepted their relationship with God as a natural thing, and turned to Him for consolation in their moment of tragedy. I myself attended private religious schools, including a Jesuit college, where the belief system I had absorbed from my parents was strengthened through a highly intellectual examination of the basic tenents of my faith in an atmosphere in which God's presence was taken for granted. (I recall sitting in class awaiting a term exam in classics. It was a small class, perhaps fourteen students in all. I tilted my head forward, closed my eyes, and folded my hands, and said a prayer. The professor, an elderly priest with thick white hair and a twinkle in his eyes, interrupted my meditation. "Frederic," he said, "if you haven't prepared, no amount of prayer will help you." I had prepared.)

For too many young people, however, spirituality is notably absent from everyday life. Not that there isn't a hunger for something more, a meaning to life. These are the years that are hallmarked by the search for meaning. But unless they see themselves as part of a community of acceptable beliefs, they can be extremely vulnerable to a wide variety of pressures ranging from an indifference to spirituality or embracing materialistic philosophies to dabbling in the occult or being drawn into a cult that promises them a certainty they have been unable to find elsewhere. As theologian and metaphysician Frithjof Schuon wrote in Des Stations de la Sagesse: " . . . there is no possible spiritual way outside of the great orthodox traditional ways. A meditation or concentration practiced at random and outside of tradition will be inoperative, and even dangerous in more than one respect, the illusion of progress in the absence of real criteria is certainly not the least of these dangers."

Young adulthood. As young adults, men and women often put spiritual concerns in the background of otherwise busy lives, pursuing careers, making money, dating, getting married, having children; returning to their religious origins long enough for a wedding, baptism, bar mitzvah, or other symbolic rites that they often perceive as primarily that—rituals to mark significant happenings.

Frequently, they're not really in touch with death, unless they work in the health professions, are policemen, firemen, or morticians. If you don't have to think about death, there's less of a need to be concerned about anything that might exist beyond this world. Because modern medicine has so greatly expanded the life span, they can prolong a sense of their own invulnerability; many don't have to face the death of parents until they themselves are well into middle age. They certainly don't have to take cemetaries too seriously. In fact, they seldom have to see them, unless they live in small towns—or on an island like Anguilla where there is a cemetary, next to a Methodist church, on top of a small hill overlooking the harbor at Road Bay. Whenever I drive past it, which is fairly often since it's on the island's one main road, and watch people of all ages pass by on their way to work or school and see the many beautiful fresh flowers placed on the graves, I think how much death is a part of life for these very religious people.

The middle years. As we reach our fifties, life seems to take on a new texture. For those who have cultivated their spirituality through the years, much as one would water and fertilize a garden, this period can represent a time of positive reappraisal and the opportunity for further enrichment. This is especially so for men and women who have persevered in their faith when they have been challenged by tragedy and have prevailed thanks to both psychological and spiritual resilience.

However, there are many who have been defeated by losses, reverses, betrayals, plain old tough times, or deceived by the trappings of material success, and who arrive at this stage in life with tattered remnants of their former spirituality, if they were ever spiritual at all. For some, there is no going back and no going forward. The light of faith burns low or may have been extinguished altogether. Here, then, is a call to search, to find it again, or perhaps to discover faith for the very first time.

In his 1946 novel, *So Little Time*, Pulitzer Prize winning author John P. Marquand captures the spiritual hunger of this phase of life. Jeffrey Wilson has left his small hometown in Massachusetts to seek his fortune in the exciting field of advertising in New York, just after the Second World War. He is very successful, moving now in a whirlwind of witty conversation, sophistication, and worship of the almighty dollar. But as he reaches his fiftieth birthday, Jeffrey is overcome with a sense of futility. He feels he has accomplished nothing meaningful in his life, and he is obsessed with the notion that time, his time, is fast running out.

In the book's final pages, Jeffrey feels a strong desire to get away from the noise and frenzy of his life and to find a moment of quiet repose. On Fifth Avenue, across from his office, is St. Patrick's Cathedral. Perhaps there, Jeffrey thought, he might find peace.

Entering, he stood part way down the main aisle, awkwardly, alone, a stranger "looking at the candles on the high altar, listening to echoed foot-steps and whispered prayers. It was not entirely for him because he was not of the Catholic faith. Some instinct, derived perhaps from his Protestant childhood at Bragg, made Jeffrey faintly suspicious of all the symbols; and yet . . . There was something in that building which had also been in Chartres, and he remembered what it had been. There was no sense of time. Although the scent of incense and the burning wax from all the candles spoke of time, still time did not disturb him."

Twilight. Being a physician, death is no stranger to me. I've seen people without any formal religious faith and little hope in an after-life grow old well and die as nobly as they lived. I've seen a couple of men who, having lived lives with little or no faith, suddenly, as if shocked by the approach of old age and especially the spectre of death, reach out to God, pray, beg forgiveness, and ask for salvation. In one of Christ's parables, did He not say that those who came later to work in the vineyards would be rewarded the same as those who had been there from the start of the day?

I like to think that the men and women in their sixties, seventies, and eighties, who seem to greatly outnumber the young at church services, are only the tip of the iceberg. Perhaps they have more time. Perhaps they feel a deeper need. Perhaps they are afraid. Perhaps they are wiser in the ways of the world and of God. Perhaps their prayers have special force. Perhaps the young, many of whom I know to possess no less intrinsic faith and sometimes more, are biding their time, waiting for their turn to make their basic confidence in God more manifest.

SPIRITUAL NUMBING

Mankind has always lived in perilous times. It's only that the perils have assumed different forms. Perhaps our times are perilous in a way no others have been. For now mankind possesses the instruments of its total annihilation.

You'd think this would produce a mad rush to God. But perhaps too many of us suffer with what psychiatrist Robert Jay Lifton has called "psychic numbing," a response to the threat of human extinction that may be accompanied by a numbing of the spirit as well.

We all realize that in this crazy and often bestial world, nuclear war is far from an impossibility. You might even say that it would be a miracle if it doesn't happen. Dr. Lifton interviewed the survivors of Hiroshima who described being aware of everything, people dying in the most grotesque ways, but then quickly feeling nothing, an acute form of psychic numbing. Over time, this numbing gave way to expressions of apathy, constriction, withdrawal, depression, even despair.

"For us to function on an everyday basis, something like a numbing process must always be operative . . . blocking the creation and re-creation of images and forms—which we may call the formative or symbolizing process . . . The other aspect of psychic numbing is the absence of existing images through which to understand unprecedented events."

While Dr. Lifton's observations are directed primarily at the psyche, they have no less powerful implications for the spirit. Consider these consequences. We can no longer be certain of descendants; our connection with prior generations is also likely to be threatened. Even the belief in immortality is affected by imagery of extinction. Of the Hiroshima experience, Lifton notes: "The hibakushas found it very hard—most cases, quite impossible—to call forth religious imagery (in their case Buddhist, Shinto, or Christian) that would help them in some way find meaning in what they had been through." *He adds that part of the problem lay in a relatively weak state of religious symbolism among an essentially secular contemporary people.*

Psychic and spiritual numbing can rob us of our enthusiasm and joy in life and of the will to make things work, like relationships and marriage. Or we may go to the other extreme, reacting with a frenzy of activity—building bigger and bigger financial empires and trophy houses to go with them—in a hedonistic pursuit of pleasure in the face of time rapidly running out. This is indeed both a material and spiritual crisis for us all, one that can be mastered only by remaining alert to the dangers, doing all we can to prevent them from becoming an actuality, and enlisting God's aid on our behalf.

TRAUMATIC EVENTS AND SPIRITUALITY

Life is rarely a smooth path, as most of us already know. Major changes, traumas, and tragedies that befall us, often at least expected moments, are critical challenges to our spirituality. In moments like these, we can as readily lose what faith we have as discover or redis-cover the importance of a relationship with God.

The very same experiences that affect our psyches can play havoc with our beliefs.

"I stopped believing in any God in Viet Nam," one patient told me. "How any God could permit that horror to happen is beyond me. You'd have to have been there to understand." Or again, a man in his late thirties, torn apart emotionally by divorce, said: "I used to go to church. I used to pray. I tried to do the right thing. Now this happens. Don't tell me there's anyone up there listening." A forty-year-old man who has just lost his wife to breast cancer shakes his head and asks what there is to believe in. A priest, profoundly disil-lusioned by the politics within his church, expresses serious doubts over whether he has chosen the right vocation, in fact, whether his faith in God has been unfounded all along. Even as He was dying on the cross, Christ exclaimed, "My God, my God, why have you for-saken me?"

A close friend of mine, a minister, called my attention to the film, *Shadowlands*, which tells the story of C. S. Lewis' brief marriage to an American named Joy. She is dying of bone cancer. Lewis is so overwhelmed by her suffering and the prospect of her death that he finds himself unable to talk with her about it. Finally, she takes him by the hand and gently pleads with him that if he will not share her suffering with her, the loneliness of her dying will be unbearably painful, that if God is in the victory after death, then God must be also in the dying. She says: "The pain now is part of the joy later. That's the deal!"

Lewis is drawn into the shadowland of her dying. As they share the pain and the fear and sorrow with each other, they also share their hope and laughter. In his journal, Lewis records: "Once very near the end I said [to Joy], 'If you can—if it is allowed—come to me when I too am on my death bed' 'Allowed!' she cried, 'Heaven would have a job to hold me; and as for Hell, I'd break it into bits.'

After Joy died, C.S. Lewis was plunged into a state of intense grief. In the past, he'd often written about pain, sorrow, and loss, and always with insight and sensitivity. But he had not actually experienced them, so his explanations were too neat and tidy to comfort him in his actual loss. The pain of his wife's death tore at his spirit until he thought he would die from it. The God about whom he had so often written in familiar terms seemed not only to have gone away some-where, but seemed to slam the door in his face and mock his life as a teacher of the Christian faith.

Slowly he came to understand that the answer to the pain of grief is in the pain itself, that by its very anguish he learned the precious-ness of love. Once he stopped cursing the dark, he found God was there in new and unexpected and wonderful ways.

Lewis was spiritually resilient. He could go through his "dark night of the soul" and emerge with renewed faith, stronger than he had been before. Conversions to faith frequently occur as a result of life crises. Some Christians refer to it as being born again. Whether such turbu-lent events as divorce or the death of your Joy damage your spiritual-ity or enrich it will be, in no small measure, determined by how spiritually resilient you are.

SOME GUIDELINES FOR STRENGTHENING OUR SPIRITUAL RESILIENCE

• *Know how to protect your spiritual self-esteem and to restore it when you have done or not done something to compromise it.* You need to have a decent appraisal of your own worth and that of everyone else too, fundamentally rooted in the value that God has placed upon us all. You must also possess operative mechanisms to restore your self-esteem when it's been damaged by guilt. There's nothing like guilt to dampen one's spirit and makes one feel ashamed. Try repentance. Humbly and with sincerity ask God's forgiveness, which He so readily gives.

• *Be willing to forgive others as you expect to be forgiven yourself.* This is one of the most important components of spiritual resilience. It's how we can model ourselves after God Himself. Forgiveness is the only way to avoid the deadly trap of bitterness and resentment, which corrode both psyche and soul. A friend of mine referred to forgiveness as a miracle in its own right, since so many people she knew, including many who professed to have religious faith, have so much trouble doing it. To forgive is to let go of hurt and anger. Easier said than done? Not if you practice the art of forgiving. Understanding the frailty of human beings and nurturing a capacity to empathize with their own difficulties and frustrations, even their susceptibility to evil, will help you to distance yourself from the wounds they may have inflicted upon you. And keep in mind that when you forgive, you do so for your own sake! This is part of your psychological and spiritual reintegration following any episode of disruption, whether you are responding to a small slight, like not being invited to a friend's party when you think you should have been, or a more grievous one, like being betrayed by a person you love. Forgiveness is the process that enables you to create a new, stronger, more insightful, and more faith-filled equilibrium. Nor does this mean that you must continue in a relationship that has been compromised. You may or you may not choose to do so. God's forgiveness always reestablishes our relationship with Him. But we humans have a right and a responsibility to decide for ourselves whether any particular relationship deserves to go on, and, if so, upon what terms it shall exist.

• *Build up your spiritual self-confidence and a healthy autonomy.* Your relationship with God is a matter of choice. You must be able to take responsibility for your own life, even though this may make you feel quite anxious at times. Avoiding this choice can only serve to activate what Paul Tillich described as "existential guilt." Denying our capacity to make choices is a form of living "inauthentically," and can generate a feeling of having betrayed ourselves. Anyone can reach out to God and surrender himself to His will, but this is ever so much more an act of free will for the person who authentically believes in himself. And only one who can experience dependency without being frightened or overwhelmed by it can feel spiritually comfortable. Consider the man or woman who is excessively dependent and fearful of the disapproval of others. Whatever its genesis—an overprotected or love-deprived childhood, failure to separate oneself from parental domination, an insecurity that seeks continual solace and reassurance—the fear can only compromise that person's spirituality. I've known a few people who are so pathologically dependent on God that they suffer miserably as the slightest moral infraction. I've known others who expect so much of God that they are invariably disappointed and disillusioned. Rabbi Harold S. Kushner reminds us of the danger of being immaturely dependent on and having unrealistic expectations about God, especially when it comes to prayers for healing. It's easy for such people to feel that, in answer to the question of why they did not get what they prayed for, it was because they didn't deserve it, or they didn't pray hard enough, or because God doesn't listen to prayers, or because there is no God. We should not, Kushner asserts, "ask God to change laws of nature for our benefit. We need only turn to Him, admit that we can't do this on our own, and understand that bravely bearing up under long-term illness is one of the most human, and one of the most godly, things we can ever do. One of the things that constantly reassures me that God is real, and not just an idea that religious leaders made up, is the fact that people who pray for strength, hope, and courage so often find resources of strength, hope, and courage that they did not have before they prayed."

• *Exercise spirituality through prayer.* It takes discipline to develop a habit of prayer. Spiritual strength is analogous to physical strength. Working out makes a big difference. Unlike the football field, however, where, if we're out of shape, we'll pay a sturdy price, in spiritual matters we're dealing with a God known for his love and mercy, who will reach out to help us even if we are spiritually flabby. And there are so many ways to pray. Formally. Informally. By yourself. With others at home. With others in a community of believers. Prayer is a universal human experience. The Lord's Prayer. The Islamic salat, performed with clock-like regularity five times every day to acknowledge God's Oneness and sovereignty on earth. Prayer that humbly acknowledges our gratitude for Creation. Native American chants that proclaim reverence of life (the very same idea which flashed into the mind of Albert Schweitzer in his little boat on the Ogowe river in Africa). Navajo artist Carl Gorman, put it this way: "It has been said by some researchers into Navajo religion that we have no Supreme God because He is not named. That is not so. The Supreme Being is not named because He is unknowable. He is simply the Unknown Power. We worship him through His Creation. We feel too insignificant to approach directly in prayer that Great Power that is incomprehensible to man. Nature feeds our soul's inspiration and so we approach Him through that Part of

Him which is close to us and within the reach of human understanding. We believe that this great unknown power is everywhere in His creation. The various forms of creation have some of
this spirit within them . . . As every form has some of the intelligent spirit of the Creator, we cannot but have reverence for all
parts of the creation."

• *Take care not to presume upon God's goodness.* He has given us the
means to deal with our lives here on earth, and many more gifts
are yet to be revealed to us. He expects us to use these wisely and
well, and allow Him to decide when, where, how, and why He
will work miracles. The Book of Sirach, describes what many
Jewish people believed in the days shortly before the birth of Jesus. Its insights are as relevant now as then:

*Hold the physician in honor, for he is essential to you, and God it was
who established his profession. From God the doctor has his wisdom . . .
God makes the earth yield healing herbs which the prudent man
should not neglect . . . God's creative work continues without cease in
its efficacy on the surface of the earth. My son, when you are ill, delay not, but pray to God who will heal you: Flee wickedness; let your
hands be just, cleanse your heart of every sin; Offer your sweet-
smelling oblation and petition, a rich offering according to your
means. Then give the doctor his place lest he leave; for you need him
too. There are times that give him an advantage, and he too beseeches
God that his diagnosis may be correct and his treatment bring about
a cure.* Sir 38:1–15.

• *Be a friend to God as He is to you.* The connectedness that Native
Americans feel with living creatures—animals, birds, all of nature—gives them a sense of familiarity in their relationship with
the Creator. These are their friends. How much more so is the In-
carnation of God in the person of Christ! Believing Jesus to be
both human and divine, Christians can not only worship God,
but also befriend Him in a very special way. Of course, to do this,

we must be well versed in those attitudes and skills required for successful interpersonal relationships. Trust, in as much as He is always there for us like a good friend. Patience and tolerance, as when your prayers are not answered in the way you had hoped them to be. Openness of communication, as when we speak with Him, to thank Him, to ask His pardon, to ask His help and guidance, to seek His compassion which is evident in His words and His miraculous healings. In this best of all friendships, we must do all we can not to betray our hope in Him as He would never betray His hope in us. And, of course, He told us what friendship is all about when he said, simply, that we should love God and love others as we love ourselves. The spiritually resilient person must be able to love, at all levels, in all ways, growing in this gift all through life so that, in our final days, we can know the depth of love that passed, for instance, between C. S. Lewis and his wife and experience the same richness of love in our friendship with God.

• *Seek to learn more about loving all through your life.* There's always more to learn. I'm still learning about love, after all these years. I remember, as a child, taking for granted that I knew what love was when I thought I loved my parents and felt secure in their love for me, most of the time. I thought I knew what love was when I had a crush on the girl who lived next door. I thought I knew what love was when I married and assumed that I'd be leading a conflict-free life with my wife and children. But it was only in the dark hours that I really came to understand more about love—no one knows all there is to know—the relief of forgiveness, the joy of reconciliation, the shared pain and compassion for the suffering of others. Over time, love became manifest in intimacies and understanding, expressed in hundred of little acts and remembrances, solidified in the friendship, the give and take, its steadiness at times when romance grows faint, its peaks of joy. I learned to wish everyone well, without exception, particularly those good people who reached out to me in my time of need and those who came to me in theirs. And although my concept of God slowly grew from one of fear and awe to one that recognized His deep concern for me and all of us, only now have I begun to really appreciate that love is at the heart of my relationship to Him and His to me.

It's the final scene of *The Miracle Worker*. ANNIE and HELEN
are alone in the yard.

> *Annie has found Helen's hand, almost without knowing it,*
> *and she spells slowly into it, her voice unsteady,*
> *whispering:*

Annie: I, love, Helen.
> *(She clutches the child to her, tight this time, not*
> *spelling, whispering into her hair.)*

> *Forever, and —*

> *(She stops. The lights over the pump are taking on*
> *the color of the past, and it brings Annie's head up,*
> *her eyes opening, in fear; and as slowly as though*
> *drawn she rises, to listen, with her hand on Helen's*
> *shoulders, slowly here, slowly there: and hears only*
> *silence. There are no voices. The color passes on, and*
> *when her eyes come back to Helen she can breathe*
> *the end of her phrase without fear:)*

> *—ever—*

Selected References

Anderson, Joan Webster. *Where Miracles Happen*. Ballantine Books, New York, 1994

Bowker, John. *The Oxford Dictionary of World Religions*. Oxford University Press, New York, 1997

Brown, Joseph Epes. *The Spiritual Legacy of the American Indian*. Crossroad, New York, 1982

Carper, Jean. *Miracle Cures*. HarperPerennial, New York, 1998

Carrel, Alexis. *The Voyage to Lourdes*. Real-View-Books, Fraser MI, 1994/ HarperCollins, New York, 1950

Catechism of the Catholic Church. Doubleday, New York, 1995

Chesterton, G. K. *Orthodoxy*. Doubleday, New York, 1990

Connell, Janice T. *Meetings with Mary*. Ballantine, New York, 1995

Debre, Patrice (trans. Forster, Elborg). *Louis Pasteur*. Johns Hopkins University Press. Baltimore, MD, 1998

De Chardin, Pierre Teilhard. *The Phenomenon of Man*. HarperCollins, New York, 1980

Dossey Larry. *Healing Words*. HarperCollins, New York, 1993

DuBos, Rene. *Celebrations of Life*. McGraw Hill, New York, 1981

Flach, Frederic. *Resilience*. Fawcett Columbine, New York, 1988. Revised edition Hatherleigh Press, New York, 1997

Flach, Frederic. *The Secret Strength of Angels*. Hatherleigh Press, New York, 1998

Fowler, James W. *Stages of Faith*. HarperCollins, New York, 1981

Geivett, R. Douglas, Habermas, Gary R. *In Defense of Miracles*. InterVarsity Press, Downers Grove, IL. 1997

Gibson, William. *The Miracle Worker*. Atheneum, New York 1960/ Bantam edition 1975

Goodall, Jane. *Reason for Hope.* Warner Books, New York, 1999

Graham, Billy. *The Holy Spirit.* Word Publishing, Dallas TX, 1988

Groeschel, Rev. Benedict J. *A Still Small Voice.* Ignatius Press, San Francisco, CA, 1992

Grossarth-Maticek, Ronald and Eysenck, H.J. "Psychological Factors in the Treatment of Cancer and Coronary Heart Disease", *Issues in Modern Therapy.* Hatherleigh Press, 1996

Joly, Eugene. *What is Faith.* Hawthorn Books, New York, 1958

Jung, C. J. *Psychology and Religion.* Yale University Press, 1992

Keutzer, Carolin S. *"Synchronicity Awareness in Psychotherapy"*, *Directions in Psychiatry,* Vol 6. Hatherleigh, New York, 1986.

Koenig, Harold G. *"Spirituality and Remission of Depression in Medically Ill Older Patients"*, *Directions in Psychiatry,* Vol 18, Hatherleigh, New York, 1998

Kushner, Harold S. *When Bad Things Happen to Good People.* Avon Books, New York, 1981

Lacey, Robert and Danziger, Danny. *The Year 1000. What Life Was Like at the Turn of the First Millennium.* Little Brown and Company, Boston, 1999

Lifton, Robert Jay. *"The Psychologic Impact of the Threat of Extinction,"* *Directions in Psychiatry,* Vol 1, Hatherleigh, New York, 1981

C. S. Lewis. *Miracles.* Simon and Schuster, New York, 1996

Lourdes Sanctuary. Internet: www.lourdes-france.com

MacNutt, Francis. *Healing.* Ave Maria Press, Notre Dame, IN 1974/1996

MacNutt, Francis. *The Power to Heal.* Ave Maria Press, Notre Dame, IN, 1997

Meissner, W.W. *"The Pathology of Belief Systems"*, *Directions in Psychiatry*, Vol. 11, Hatherleigh, New York,1991

The New Oxford Annotated Bible with the Aprocrypha/New Revised. Oxford University Press, 1994

Peale, Norman Vincent. *The Power of Positive Thinking* Fawcett. Columbine,New York, 1996

Peale, Norman Vincent and Blanton, Smiley. *Faith Is the Answer.* Prentice-Hall, New York, 1950

Peck, M. Scott. *People of the Lie.* Simon and Schuster, New York, 1997

Pickering, George. *Creative Malady.* Oxford Univ. Press, New York, 1977

Porter, Roy. *The Greatest Benefit to Mankind.* W.W. Norton, New York, 1997

Siegal, Bernie. *Love, Medicine, and Miracles: Lessons Learned About Self-Healing from a Surgeon's Experience with Exceptional Patients.* HarperPerennial, San Francisco, 1990

Schweitzer, Albert. *Reverence for Life.* Irvington Pub, 1993

Trotta, Liz. *Jude: A Pilgramage to the Saint of Last Resort.* HarperSanFrancisco, 1998

Wager, Susan. *A Doctor's Guide to Therapeutic Touch.* Berkley Publishing, New York, 1996

Warner, Wayne E. *Kathryn Kuhlman: The Woman Behind the Miracles.* Servant Publications, Ann Arbor, MI, 1993

Weil, Andrew. *Spontaneous Healing: How to Discover and Enhance Your Body's Natural Ability to Maintain and Heal Itself.* Knopf, New York, 1995

Weisner, Irving S. *"The Clinical Exploration of the Patient's World View,"* *Directions in Psychiatry* Vol. 16, Hatherleigh, New York, 1996

Index

The author is grateful to the following for permission to quote passages from copyrighted material.

About the Author

Dr. Frederic Flach graduated summa cum laude from St. Peter's College, where he majored in philosophy. He received his medical degree from Cornell University Medical College. He has practiced psychiatry for more than forty years. He was awarded a papal knighthood in The Equestrian Order of the Knights of the Holy Sepulchre of Jerusalem in 1999. Sir Frederic has always been vitally interested in the relationship between faith, health, and the quality of life. He is married and has five children and six grandchildren.